Mental Health In A Failed American System

What Every Parent, Family

and

Caregiver Should Know

Támara Hill, MS

Library of Congress Cataloging in Publication Data
Library of Congress Control Number
2013915043
Hill-Sage Press
ISBN-10: 0615870325
ISBN-13: 978-0615870328

Table of Contents

Preface

According to the National Center for Children In Poverty (2013), 20% of adolescents have a diagnosable mental health disorder, while 34.2 million live in low-income households, which means little to no income for mental health treatment. About 7.7 million adults and 20% of children and teens between 13 and 18 suffer from severe mental illness. Suicide is the 3rd leading cause of death among 15-24 year olds, even on college campuses as well. According to the National Institute of Mental Health (2013), about 5.7 million adults age 18+ suffer from bipolar disorder each year, while major depression has become the leading cause of disability in the United States for individuals ages 15-24. Even more, 24-million suffer from schizophrenia, 40 million suffer from anxiety disorders each year, and 7.7 million suffer from post-traumatic stress disorder in any given year. As you can see, we are in an epidemic. We need treatment and hope.

Mental health, lack of resources, and attention to parents are the most controversial topics of the modernity of times. Multiple reports on mental health and local meetings or protests regarding changes in policy, infiltrate our lives almost daily. A call for greater attention to mental health occurred during late 2012 following a cascade of violent acts involving schizophrenia, bipolar disorder, and other severe mental illnesses requiring adequate treatment. We have quite a history demanding our attention: Seung-Hui Cho (killed 32, wounded 17 on the campus of Virginia Tech in 2007), Jared Loughner (attempted murder in Tucson Arizona, seriously wounding former Senator Gabrielle Giffords in 2011), James Holmes (mass shooter at Century movie theater in Aurora Colorado in 2012), William Spengler (murderer of his grandmother in 1980 and gunman who ambushed firefighters in 2012), Adam Lanza (Newtown Connecticut, Sandy Cook elementary school shooting in 2012), Jimmy Dykes (held 5-

year-old boy hostage in underground bunker in 2013), and Michael Brandon Hill (packing 500 rounds of ammunition in a Georgia Elementary school). While these horrific incidents reflect a small proportion of cases involving mental illness, they emphasize the serious consequences of failing to treat the most vulnerable in our society. We need to apply pressure to politicians, useless hospital policies, and outmoded state laws that create heartache for families of suffering loved ones. Unfortunately, society is held hostage by fear of creating more stigma by pointing things out. Fear holds society back from advocating long lasting changes in state laws. Despite frequent attempts at changing current policies, resistance meets families desperate to change mediocre mental health protocols and policies that offer no recourse in severe cases of mental health. Resistance comes disguised as protection of civil liberties or freedom of speech. As a result, many parents, families, and caregivers feel defeated by the majority of Americans who strive to maintain the current rules of society. But for families who live in the jaws of fear each day because of life with a loved one with a severe or untreated mental illness, change must occur soon. Protection of their loved one outweighs anything else. Because families are often unable to influence wider social change, it is important that they learn ways to help themselves within their community. Another major problem is confidentiality and HIPAA laws. Many families are barred from helping their loved ones.

This book is about the challenges you will encounter in a system dominated by hidden forces, political power, firm resistance, and even well-meaning changes in policy. Our system is mainly dominated by politics and social influence. This book was designed to provide information about the major problems parents, families, and caregivers face and offer resources, suggestions, and avenues to take. I encourage you to see this book as a companion. A companion you can use to help you research, evaluate, and seek out information. I hope this book is motivation for you to question, research, and evaluate every avenue you are likely to take.

Acknowledgements

$\mathcal{I}$ am a firm believer in the power of showing humility and gratitude. These two qualities are often missing in our daily lives, so I want to exercise them here. One empowering force in my life is my relationship with my mother. Having dedicated herself to home-education, gypsy lifestyle to expose me and my siblings to the world, and walking side-by-side me through higher education and multiple media engagements, I am eternally grateful to God for giving me such a wonderful mom. I can honestly say that she has planted seeds in my life. Thank you for reading many of my drafts and helping me to envision success for this book. May God continue to bless you mom. To my grandmother, thank you for your support. Every prayer matters in my life. May God continue to bless you too.

I want to thank my brother for his wonderful editing and technology skills. Your input and artistic perspective has added great value to this project. Your patience has been a representation of your character. Good things are coming your way soon.

It is also proper that I thank you, the reader, for picking up this book and taking the first step into your future with the knowledge that has revolutionized my perception of this field. I hope this book will be a start to becoming independent and developing the courage you need to tackle one of the biggest systems in the world.

Hang on…we'll get to the finish line together!

Tamara Hill

The only medicine for suffering, crime, and all other woes of mankind is wisdom.

Thomas Huxley

Mental Health In A Failed American System

What Every Parent, Family

and

Caregiver Should Know

Introduction

ental health care is one of the most emotionally charged topics of our day. There are multiple concerns among families everywhere regarding mental health treatment. Unanswered questions, fears, worry, guilt, and uncertainty characterize families and caregivers who have a loved one with a mental health problem or even special need. Parents I have spoken to often end up crying, experiencing denial, researching every piece of information nonstop only to later feel even more confused, or reaching out to anyone who seems to have a ready-made answer or remedy for the pain. Ready-made cures don't exist; neither do answers to some of your unanswered questions. An acceptance of this fact is the first step toward emotional healing. The good news is that there is hope and some of that hope is found in the tools and chapters you will encounter in this book.

There are probably various questions that invade your mind and heart daily as a family member or caretaker. Questions about the type of mental health setting your loved one may need, whether medication should be accepted or rejected, what type of medication fits your loved one's needs, what to question and what not to question, how to find a therapist and what to look for, and what legal options you have and don't have. Families and caregivers remain oblivious to the mental health system and often rely solely on professionals to enlighten them and guide them through the system. This is a mistake. The reality is that the mental health system is unable to dedicate such time to families and caregivers, often leaving them all alone. Ultimately, it will be your responsibility to learn about the system and protect those you love. The best way to protect yourself and your loved one is to learn as much as you can. Parents, families, and caregivers are a "minority" group in the mental health system. With a lack of healthcare providers understanding their core issues, insurance coverage, and long waiting lists, this population is hungry for knowledge, direction, and peace of mind. The first step toward these things is embracing truth about our "fallen" mental health system and following hard after what I refer to as self-knowledge. Self-knowledge is knowledge that you pursue on your own time, for your own benefit, and for the benefit of those you love. This type of knowledge is not simple repetition and reciting of facts that others teach us, but rather the search for truth by comparing information, pondering the basis of information, and questioning its validity. It's a treasure hunt for truth. Gaining knowledge is not a passive endeavor, it is an active process of understanding the world around us. Self-knowledge precedes empowerment. Ways to empower yourself will be further discussed in chapter 1.

Families often yell loud for state and federal reform, yet nothing happens. They fight harder for attention through the media, yet nothing happens. They write their legislators and Senators while holding fast to the efforts of mental health conglomerates, and still nothing happens. Many continue to ask "what will it take and whose voice will finally be heard?" We continue to struggle with systemic options that are outmoded and ineffective. As a therapist, I find myself feeling that mental health professionals are not doing enough. I often ponder what more I can do to change or enhance the system. Sometimes it feels like humanity is too "small" to battle such a large system. Thankfully, we have a few social warriors who are standing strong and fighting for the benefit of those who cannot fight for themselves. Resources are available to help guide you but you must first know where to find them and how to use them appropriately. This book will help empower you to navigate the mental health system a little better with confidence.

We should not wait until life strikes us to stand for what is right, but often this is the case. It wasn't until a 26-year-old male murdered his grandmother, without warning in Richland Township Pennsylvania in February of 2013, that many began applying pressure to PA state officials to change civil commitment laws and outmoded hospital policies. Outdated civil commitment laws, nonsensical state laws, and vast support of the "dangerousness" criteria to be admitted to a psychiatric hospital involuntarily, has led to repeated national tragedies. For example, in many states, an adolescent as young as 14 or 16 years old can make legal decisions on their mental health treatment. The older a child becomes, the harder it is to know about what's going on with treatment. If a14-year-old (e.g., in Pennsylvania) or adult does not believe they need treatment, they can refuse it. The most a therapist can do is try to encourage and motivate that individual to give treatment a try. Most advocates, grass-roots organizations, mental health professionals, and behavioral health researchers cringe at the above horrifying story and many others like it. But long before these types of stories, society took a bad hit as a result of what is known as de-institutionalization (the process of reducing long-term care). This process has jumpstarted a cascade of catastrophes that have included but are not limited to victimization, homelessness, violence, homicide, and incarceration across the nation. What is very disheartening for families is that society and mental health professionals tend only to think in-depth about protocols, treatment, and changing laws when something tragic occurs close to home. It is usually when the tragedy greets us at home and the fear of violence strikes at our innermost being that we become proactive. Full discussion of these dilemmas will continue in chapter 2 and 4. Sadly, the process of reforming the mental health system never includes the complaints that families and caregivers have regarding a need for increased access to resources, treatment, education, and financial support. Reform has continued to ignore the basic needs of families and suffering individuals with severe mental illness (SMI) or even special needs. The presuming social view that mental illness is not as serious as the media says it is, blocks progress. This is largely political. The less we look at severe mental illness, the less stigma we experience and the fewer people advocate for flexible treatment options. The goal of most recovery campaigns or advocacy groups is to increase autonomy of sufferers. But changes need to occur for vulnerable populations who aren't so independent.

While a student of psychology in higher education, I felt a part of a social movement to study human behavior and advocate for better access to treatment. I believed I was entering a field that was hard pressed to see universal consensus and make real, lasting changes. But I was largely mistaken. No one really cared. The haunting reality is that we live in a contemporary, techno-driven society that remains largely uninformed about mental health, even in higher education. Despite wide-spread media coverage of mental health problems, society sweeps the issue under the rug and tends to address more socially understood constructs such as gun law restrictions, stigma, and social justice. This wide-spread lack of public support and social democracy has been a negative contributing factor to proper attention to mental health for centuries. Sadly, this same nonchalant attitude fills our universities. Politicization of mental health not only affects the public sector nationwide, but our educational system and developing professionals. As a hopeful, perhaps even naive student some years ago, my perceptions were based on the few compassionate professionals I had seen in operation in the field. But in reality, mental health had become a very controversial, politically laced, angry field. Psychology and counseling students are not introduced to the politics that has created landmines for professionals and families pursuing it. So many students hold false perceptions until they enter the field. Once in the field, they have little to no interest in changing things. They become complacent and highly influenced, failing to become agents of change. They become part of the problem. Even still, it appears that as each year goes by, as policies change, and as new generations infiltrate the field with cultural and social ideologies, the mental health system continues to undergo drastic reform but never completely in a positive direction. For example, the development of the Diagnostic and Statistical Manual of Mental Disorders, 4th edition, Text Revision (DSM-IV-TR) has undergone repeated revisions, not so much due to research and scientific knowledge, but rather social influence and the "majority rule." The DSM is influenced by the political views of elite researchers, psychiatrists, and other healthcare professionals who are chosen to get together in a group known as the Work-Group during a series of planned conferences and meetings. Diagnostic criteria, new labels, and uses for the labels are developed to fit the leading socially constructed, politically charged theories of society. In late 2012, the DSM-5 (also known as DSM-V) Work-Group reached an agreement in the design and agreed to label frequent temper tantrums that occur three or more times per week, among youths ages 6-18, Disruptive Mood Dysregulation Disorder. Critics emerged from the woodwork to criticize what appears to be the biggest caricature of the field of psychiatry in history. A historical as well as modern day review of the DSM will be covered in more depth in chapter 3. Nonetheless, I soon found out that there was an insidious battle between "experts" on everything such as research, statistical findings, parenting, treatment, normalcy, abnormal behavior, bullying prevention, children with special needs, treatment of SMI, managed healthcare, grassroots movements, advocacy, how to interact with clients, and how to implement state-wide civil commitment laws. We never agree. A continuing battle between mental health professionals and civil rights attorneys, organizations, and advocates continue to create firm resistance to implementing potentially beneficial programs in states where individuals cannot care for themselves. For example, while 44 states accept court-ordered treatment (when the law orders patients to get treatment), Connecticut and Maryland do not, making it difficult to get a severely impaired individual the help they need. A person, severely impaired, who cannot receive court ordered care has a grim fate including but not limited to poor decision-making, negative interactions with law enforcement, impulsivity, or violence. While court-ordered treatment may not be beneficial for everyone with a mental health diagnosis, it will be useful to some of those who do. A review of why we need systemic change and a discussion on treatment models that have been used to control SMI will be discussed in chapter 4.

As I entered the field as a beginning therapist, I thought to myself "what happened to counseling and offering services to the individual who simply needs help?" That was far from reality. I realized that my own field was dominated by politics, democracy, gate-keepers, money, insurance, and the biggest evil of all, the DSM. I was certainly in for the ride of my life and a future full of experiences that would change my perception of, but not my love for, the field forever. While we will be looking at the many problems that are inherent in the system, we will also look at the various ways in which families can cope and work around the system. Resources will be provided in most chapters.

Many individuals feel helpless when they get sucked into the system following the diagnosis of a loved one. From the moment a family receives a mental health diagnosis onward, the family must join forces with all professionals they come in contact with in order to provide the best treatment for their loved one. But what happens when that loved one, of legal age, refuses treatment and refuses to adhere to a treatment schedule? Families find themselves on their knees begging the system to hear their cries. Treating a loved one is a trial-and-error process characterized by repeated trials over time and consultations with various healthcare professionals. The field is replete with confusion and families often fold beneath the stress involved in seeking out healthcare, accepting a diagnosis, understanding what a diagnosis will mean, and living with the reality of mental impairment. Because families are often on their own to understand the system, poor treatment choices are made and families become hopeless. As a result of this continuing reality, this book was written as a resource for you. This book was also written as a resource for those I love and care about. It's a book to encourage thinking beyond what is seen and new ways to strengthen our independence. The proper treatment of your loved one will boil down to you. You should not expect the system to walk closely with you, explain every incident you encounter, and protect your loved one from danger. I liken the mental health system to that of a gas station, a stop-and-go center that gives you temporary resources so that you can navigate the road on your own. For many people approaching the system at face value, it is a place where safety and help reside. But the truth is that families are on their own. For example, they are often turned away if their loved one's illness does not meet certain criteria to be admitted to a hospital or enrolled in a school for kids with special needs. Even when families cannot afford care or insurance companies do not see a clear reason for why your loved one is receiving treatment, insurance companies will either turn you away (not accept your request for services) or stop paying for treatment. You can find resources to help with this in chapter 1. As a bonus chapter, I will offer resources for parents of children with special needs experiencing bullying.

Ultimately, you will learn about the various challenges that you are likely to encounter while seeking help in a system dominated by hidden forces. While there are mental health professionals in the field who genuinely seek to understand, treat, advocate for, and support those with mental illness, there are also individuals in the field who are unable to contribute positively. Reasons for this include skewed perceptions of mental illness and human behavior, lack of compassion and unconditional positive regard, incompetence or lack of proper knowledge, or becoming overly influenced by politics, theories, and seasoned professionals. Social desire, politics, and law all converge to make seeking mental health treatment a very big challenge. As a result, I believe in do-it-yourself remedies, but first you must have the proper knowledge, the open-mind, and confidence to do it. This field is very perplexing and you don't want to go at it alone.

Chapter 1

Learning how to obtain essential information

$\mathcal{I}$nformation in this chapter is given to jumpstart your new journey toward gaining self-knowledge. As stated in the introduction, it is important that you as the parent, family, or caregiver understand things as simple as the credential and training or career experience of mental health professionals and where to seek resources and financial help. For many seeking or receiving psychiatric treatment, the assessment process or the first visit to a healthcare facility is daunting. The paperwork, the insurance, the financial out-of-pocket cost, prescription costs, regular visits, terminology, choosing the best treatment setting or provider, and bonding with a healthcare professional can all seem so overwhelming. During this process, it is important that you understand how to guard yourself from choosing the wrong healthcare provider or signing paperwork you do not fully understand. During the first visit to a psychiatric facility, your loved one (or you) will sign multiple documents, but the most important is informed consent (a form used to obtain permission to treat your loved one), confidentiality form (agreeing to terms and expectations), and authorization or release of information (permission to release, receive, or share information). The process is not only intimidating and frightening for many families, but also mentally and emotionally exhausting. You must arm yourself with knowledge beforehand. The issues briefly reviewed in this chapter will include: understanding HIPAA (Health Insurance Portability and Accountability Act of 1996) and confidentiality, confusion over a professional's credentials and level of education, unfamiliarity with what is known as a theoretical orientation, fear of financial cost and strain, and lack of information regarding free and low-cost solutions to treatment. Some of these topics will be covered in chapter 2. But let's start with understanding credentials first.

Many people are sadly misinformed about the professional title of their healthcare provider and often do not believe that the title holds any relevance to the level of care received. The truth is that every parent, family member, or caregiver should know a little bit about the education, background, and professional experiences of their healthcare provider. Of course you wouldn't want to outright ask "where did you go to school?" "Did you pass all of your exams?" "How experienced are you?" But you simply want to ask if they can tell you a little about their background. Most providers are privy to this but be careful in how you ask. You can also scan the office walls which can tell you a lot about a person in some cases or do a Better Business Bureau check. Word of mouth is sometimes useful. Trying to understand professional titles and level of experience in the mental health field can be a daunting task itself. All the many names, abbreviations, and acronyms perplex the savviest researcher. It's okay if you aren't familiar with what BCBA (Board Certified Behavior Analysis) or LPC (License Professional Counselor) means. You can simply ask the person holding the credential or Google it.

Most of us have been to the doctor's office for routine physicals and observed a variety of abbreviated letters next to the provider's last name. As recipients of treatment you deserve to know who is treating your loved one, what level of education they received (which can offer you some information on how competent they are), and what the treatment team at a hospital, community center, or clinic actually looks like. Most experienced professionals know how to make the best decisions for their patients, design workable treatment plans and goals, and offer reputable referral services. Keep in mind that one of the most important tools of empowerment for families and caregivers is self-knowledge. When you seek treatment you need to be armed with knowledge of who might have access to treating you and what their specialty is. For example, if you decide to seek treatment at a community mental health center, you need to know that there are Bachelor level workers (4-year-college level), Master level workers (4-year-college + 2-3 years of advanced higher education), licensed workers (4-years college, 2-3 years graduate school, and 2-3 years supervision under an established professional), medical doctors or psychiatrists (4-years college + 5-8 years of graduate school) and psychologists (4-years college + 5-6 years of higher education). Those with advanced degrees usually have specialties (areas of expertise) such as child and adolescent mental health or adult post-traumatic stress disorder or psychotic disorders. There are also Master level workers who are license eligible or LPC-Interns (eligible for a license in their state after receiving 2-3 years of supervision under a professional who has over 5 years of experience as a licensed professional). These individuals provide a great deal of counseling and psychotherapy services. Many go on to open a private practice.

Let's briefly review some commonly seen degrees and their abbreviations in health care settings:

The BSW degree (Bachelor of Social Work)
- o According to the Bureau of Labor Statistics (2012), BSW programs prepare students for direct-service positions such as caseworker or mental health assistants. These programs teach students about diverse populations, human behavior, and social welfare policy. All programs require students to complete supervised fieldwork or an internship. Some employers in counseling settings hire workers who have a bachelor's degree in a related field such as sociology or social work.

The MSW degree (Master of Social Work)
- o Allows individuals with a BS or BA degree to attend 2 more years of higher education, obtain licensure, professional supervision, and practice social work independently. MSW degrees can be found in inpatient, community, and clinical settings. These individuals usually have a vast array of knowledge of social services in the community. License Clinical Social Worker (LCSW) is the professional licensure title.

The B.A. and B.S. degree (Bachelor of Arts)
- o Bachelor of Arts and Bachelor of Science degrees can be achieved at the college level, usually requiring four years of study. Individuals with these degrees can work under the supervision, often as an assistant, of a therapist with a higher degree such as the Masters degree. Think of the B.A. and B.S. degrees as offering introductory educational and work experiences in psychology. You might find yourself receiving certain services in both inpatient and outpatient settings from an individual with a bachelor's degree, but this service is usually limited and reviewed by an experienced

worker. For example, a child who is receiving therapy in an outpatient clinical setting, might initially be interviewed by phone or in person by an individual with a bachelor's degree, but later be monitored by a therapist with a "higher" degree and more experience. Most TSS (Therapeutic Staff Service) or BSC (Behavior Consultant) workers have these degrees.

The M.S. (Master of Science) and M.A. (Master of Arts) degree

o   The M.S. and M.A. degrees can be obtained in both clinical and counseling psychology. Individuals at this level spend an extra 1-2yrs in higher education (i.e., professional level of training after college), which prepares them for more advanced work in the field of psychology. The M.A. degree is very similar to the M.S. degree. These individuals could also work in the field as independent Licensed Professional Counselors (LPCs) and obtain a private practice.

The PhD (Doctor of Philosophy) and PsyD (Doctor of Psychology) degree.

o   Doctor of Philosophy (PhD) or Doctor of Psychology (PsyD) degree allows a mental health professional to hold the title of a psychologist and practice independently in their state. These degrees often require 4+ years of graduate study after the BA/BS or MS/MA degrees. These individuals can also become licensed as LPC's or LCSW's.

WHAT EVERY PARENT, FAMILY, & CAREGIVER
SHOULD KNOW

Individuals with an advanced degree (a degree beyond college) in counseling or psychotherapy usually have what is known as a theoretical orientation, which is initially evaluated in graduate school. A theoretical orientation is basically the worldview or belief system of the therapist. This dictates how a therapist will treat your loved one, conduct therapy, utilize community resources, approach family related issues, and refer to other types of treatment. You want to ask a potential therapist what his or her theoretical orientation is so that you can get an idea of the types of therapy sessions your loved one will engage in. Keep in mind when seeking a therapist that a theoretical orientation expresses beliefs regarding how the world works, how the mind and behavior works, how families engage, and types of treatment. For example, a therapist who was trained in psychodynamic counseling believes that childhood experiences have a lot of influence on adult behavior. An existential therapist believes that it is important to develop meaning and purpose in one's life and take control of their future. A behavior therapist believes that behavior can be changed by employing specific interventions (e.g., journaling, close monitoring of behavior, or reinforcement) to change negative behavior. My theoretical orientation is integrative, meaning that I integrate both behavior therapy and existential therapy. If you visit my website (Anchored-In-Knowledge) you can read more about it there (see "About author" page).

It is also important to understand who your nurse is. There are some nurses who operate under the supervision of a licensed professional counselor or social worker and provide psychiatric services, but to a limited degree. Unfortunately, in some settings, individuals are placed in positions they are not 100% qualified to perform in. But as a result of office politics (favoritism, seniority, company needs, or social ranking), there isn't really much parents, families, or caregivers can do but leave that treatment setting and pursue services that are more properly distributed.

Despite the level of education and qualifications a mental health professional has, treatment often consists of a collaborative process between the patient and healthcare provider. The therapeutic relationship is the most important component of therapy and treatment, not the degree or title the individual possesses. An individual can have the highest level of education in the land and still lack the essential qualities to provide professional services. For example, there are many psychologists and other mental health professionals who also have a national license yet have very negative bedside manners and cross many boundaries with patients (see Ringstad, 2008, in "References").

Families, parents, and caregivers should also become knowledgeable about the type of treatment they are being offered, the length of time in treatment required, and the efficacy or success rate of a particular treatment. For example, therapists will often treat depression with a treatment known as Cognitive Behavior Therapy (a type of therapy that focuses on dysfunctional thoughts and ways to alter them). Another therapist may begin treating an individual who engages in multiple suicide attempts with Dialectical Behavior Therapy (a type of therapy that focuses on teaching the client how to regulate emotional reactions). Both of these treatments have differences that you should know about. Ask the provider to explain their techniques and treatment recommendations. At any rate, the most important take away is to never be afraid to ask questions, gain better insight, and learn about the experience of a mental health professional. Always remember to do your research.

Finding resources for your family

As a mental health professional I often find myself confused, frustrated, and overwhelmed by the mental health needs of our youth today. Even with a few years of education and career experience under my belt, I still feel lost for words when a parent describes the grueling process of seeking services for her child. I find myself inwardly say a prayer in hopes that she will find her way. If I have the opportunity to be close enough to reach that person, I will. I almost "flood" a parent with resources and direction. My ultimate goal has been to offer the direction I see so many families without. I have been close enough to families to see the frustration and pain inherent in not knowing where to turn, feeling alone, and maybe even cursed. Within my own family, confusion arose at an earthshattering circumstance of a loved one and no one knew where to turn. The search for support was undermined by the strong emotions attached to the loss. I can only imagine how families of a loved one with severe mental illness feel. Whether it's coping with the death of a loved one with a mental illness or receiving an unfavorable mental health diagnosis, many people are often too depressed to research their options. Sometimes they just don't have the words to say or know what questions to ask. In severe cases, families get strung along through the mental health system hoping that someone would finally help them. What these families are often unaware of is that many mental health professionals are at the mercy of their own level of knowledge. In other words, many times mental health professionals, while quite skilled, engage in much hypothesis testing, posing questions to superiors, and scratching their heads at confusing data. In less severe cases, a mental illness can be easy to identify, but difficult to treat. In other circumstances, the right services are often not affordable, funded, or simply unavailable. Many families have been turned away because there weren't "enough beds" or that person didn't have insurance. Some people simply aren't "severe enough" to be admitted even though that person may be hallucinating or a family fears for their life. The interpretation of most families is that "I have to let my kid (or family member) threaten suicide or homicide to have them admitted?" Hospitals often say "come back to us when your loved one is on the verge of barely surviving." Heartless? Cruel? Irresponsible? Yes indeed. Thankfully there are advocates who are serious about changing this structural confusion. To name a few: The Treatment Advocacy Center (TAC), National Alliance on Mental Illness (NAMI), and Active Minds. There are times I wonder if the real "professionals" are those who have experienced a deep feeling of confusion about the field or experience the flaws of the system on a personal level. When things get close, we get real. It's an unfortunate and sad reality. But it is also a reality that has inspired advocates to speak out against it.

Even with advocates, it is important we know where to turn for help. A parent of a former client of mine had a very difficult time accessing the appropriate resources to transfer her daughter from a school known for violence. She visited every mental health coordinator in the city she knew, but did not know that the appropriate resources were an email and phone call away. There are a few general things I believe you can do to help yourself locate appropriate resources:

o Research everything: Become knowledgeable about mental health and how its "treated" in your state. Each state is different and laws dictate who gets treatment, when, and why. In the state of PA, an individual cannot be involuntarily admitted to a hospital against his/her will if the individual has not threatened the life of others or himself, even if he/she is hallucinating, unable to care for basic needs, is homeless, or in a state of severe confusion. Knowledge truly is power. Become connected with someone who understands the system so that you can gain further knowledge. The best suggestion I could give you is to gain knowledge on your own. Would you attempt to drive a car without adjusting the mirrors? No. Don't attempt to tackle the mental health field without researching it first.

o   Find emotional support: When caring for a loved one with a mental health condition, it is important to speak to others sometimes for suggestions or emotional support. Try the national New Life Live radio broadcast at 1-800-New-LIFE or 639-5433.

o   Seek out legal advocacy: AOT is court-ordered treatment (including medication) that is available in 44 states. It is often utilized with individuals who have a history of medication noncompliance. AOT is for individuals with severe mental illness who require strict maintenance. Many families advocate for the implementation of this system in their state or region.

o   Research your library: Utilize that library card that you've tossed in the corner. Local libraries have resources in social services that can give you direction. If you dig a little deeper, you can request professional books and articles through your ILL (Interlibrary Loan) service.

o   Google what you need to know: Set up Google alerts regarding mental health reform, law changes, or local mental health news. www.google.com/alerts.

o Sign up with local organizations: My Pennsylvania Psychological Association offers membership for a small fee to people outside the field. They send monthly newsletters and keep you informed about workshops or free classes for families.

o Make your case manager work: In some of my previous cases as a therapist, I had to act as a child's case worker. Many times parents are either uninformed about the benefits of case workers or believe they cannot help them as much as a therapist can. Find out who your case manager is and make them work for you. They have resources everywhere!

o Call around for clarification: HIPAA (Health Insurance Portability and Accountability Act) is difficult for most people to understand. Go to http://www.naic.org/documents/consumer_hipaare ps.pdf to find local State Insurance Department contacts.

Although help seems scarce and many holes in the system prevent families from getting proper treatment, there are ways you can protect your loved one. Unfortunately you will have to learn how to swim through the sea of confusion to get the services that should be right at your doorstep. This next section will look at ways to work around financial strain.

Cost effective ways to pursue treatment

A lot of families are unaware of the various options available to them in the mental health and social service system. The most important thing for families is financial support. Seeking mental health treatment or even having a medication filled can add up to thousands of dollars. Let's review a few options that you have to help you financially care for your loved one.

- o Supplemental Social Security Disability: Find out if your loved one qualifies for social security disability. Visit the Benefits Eligibility Tool www.benefits.gov/ssa. Try Medicaid Waivers (used by the state to help pay for services) at www.medicaid.gov.

- o Don't be afraid of legal help: Contact your local or state Bar Association for legal information regarding social security disability. The Bar Association offers free legal resources.

- o Obtain support through government: Contact the National Organization of Social Security Claim Representatives, an organization of advocates and attorneys who advocate for individuals with disabilities interested in Social Security Income. You can contact them at: www.nosscr.org. The National Association of Disability Representatives

(NADR) is a similar organization. Contact them at: www.dadr.org. If your claim is denied, you may have to contact a disability lawyer or advocate who can help you compile appropriate paperwork and present it effectively. Most families are discouraged by having to seek an attorney because they believe they are expensive. However, keep in mind that there are free legal advocates that you can contact. You can inquire about a social security attorney at the lawyer referral services of NADR at 800-431-2804.

o Sliding scales: Make sure you inquire at your healthcare facility about what is known as sliding fee scales. This "payment plan" allows you to pay a variable amount to cover your healthcare costs and depends on your overall income. Some healthcare providers fully support this while others do not. Inquire.

o Payment plans: Because of the state of our economy, many mental health therapists, career counselors, clinics, community centers, hospitals, and even summer camps are offering payment plans to lower income families. Unfortunately, not all locations will advertise their use of payment plans, so make sure that you ask ahead of time if the facility you are interested in offers payment plans.

o Free assessments: You can contact your local clinic or community mental health center to inquire about free mental health assessments. Many local agencies offer them.

Children and adolescents

It is often quite expensive for parents and families to consider seeking a therapist or mental health treatment in a free-standing clinic or agency. But there are other options for families in this dilemma:

o Try the school setting: There are "free" and government paid counseling services at your child's school. Ask around. Your child can receive individual, group, and maybe even family counseling. School counselors are also another great option. If you have trouble with lunch, ask about the National School Lunch Program, which provides lunches at no cost to you. It provides balanced, healthy lunches to more than 31 million kids. Go to: www.fns.usda.gov/slp.

o Try Nonprofits: Nonprofit organizations offer various benefits for low-income families such as sliding scales fees, funds, or mental health treatment.

o Free clinics: The National Association of Free and Charitable Clinics offers great resources and if you go to their website, you can type in your location to find a free clinic in your area. Go to: www.nafcclinics.org for further information. The U.S. Department of Health and Human Services: Health Resources and Services Administration also offers resources on federally funded clinics that provide mental health treatment. Check into: www.hrsa.gov. If you live in the state of Kansas, Two Rivers Behavioral Health System offers free mental health assessments. Go to: www.tworivershospital.com/assessment.

o Local Teaching Universities: Did you know that teaching universities offer low-cost services? Teaching universities are universities where professionals are being trained or are working under an internship. For example, the University of Pennsylvania or University of Pittsburgh offers great low-cost resources for families such as Services for Teens At Risk (STAR), which offers mental health assessments at a reduced cost or free.

o Try your job: Did you know that your Employee Assistance Program (EAP) offers you resources for mental health treatment and counseling? As long as you work for an employer who offers this program and you meet specific requirements, you can inquire about programs offered.

o Community Mental Health: Most people are uninformed about the differences between psychiatric hospitals, clinics, and community mental health settings. Community mental health settings tend to provide low-cost or free services to individuals within the community. You can find a provider at the National Council For Community Behavioral Healthcare: www.thenationalcouncil.org by clicking on "find a provider in…."

o Churches and Religious Counseling Centers: Many churches, synagogues, and religious organizations offer counseling at a low-cost or free to community members. Sadly, some churches require that you become a member, but other churches offer services to anyone in need. Inquire.

WHAT EVERY PARENT, FAMILY, & CAREGIVER SHOULD KNOW

o Finding a therapist: To find a therapist in your area, go to Psychology Today's "locate a therapist:" http://therapists.psychologytoday.com/rms/ or Therapy-Tribe at http://www.therapytribe.com/.

o Learn about programs that help pay for prescriptions: Do you find that it is becoming increasingly more difficult to pay for medications? If so, I encourage you to learn about federal programs that offer help paying for prescription medication. Organizations such as NeedyMeds or RxAssist can help you with the cost. Go to: http://www.needymeds.org/ or http://rxassist.org/. Here are a few others that may be helpful:

   o RxHope:(877)-267-0517
     https://www.rxhope.com/
   o Partnership for Prescription Assistance: http://www.pparx.org/ or (888) 477-2669. This organization also offers a free clinic locator. Go to the home page of the site, click on "prescription assistance programs," and on the left hand side you will see "free/low cost clinic finder."
   o Walmart: Go to:
     http://www.walmart.com/cp/1078664?from PageCatId=5431 to download a form of eligible prescritions for the 30-day supply of generic drugs for only $4. A 90-day supply is $10. Any participating Walmart has them.

o Check your state Medicaid Office: to determine your eligibility go to www.medicaid.gov and click on "state profiles."

Conclusion

It is really difficult for parents, families, and caregivers to secure psycho-education and other resources for their loved one. Unfortunately, therapists and other mental health professionals aren't always good curators neither are they always resourceful with their patients. This is why it is a wonderful thing when you find a therapist who knows how to make use of the best resources for your situation. In many cases, mental health professionals will fail to provide your family with information that you can actually use at home. Most therapists are good at providing in office information, but very poor at sending you away feeling empowered by things you learned in session. As a result, you will often have to be your own "therapist" by learning ways to find community-based resources and information that you and your loved one can ultimately benefit from. I encourage you to keep a listing of resources in your community in an organizer so that you can keep up with all of your resources. Caring for or living around a loved one with a severe or untreated mental illness can take its toll on you. The last thing you need is a bag or box full of information to make your life more cluttered and stressful. Organizing information will help you be better prepared to attend therapy sessions, treatment meetings, case management, support groups, and other services. You will also be more willing and prepared to provide information to people treating your loved one. Your ultimate goal is to find the tools you need, organize them, and have them when you need them most.

Chapter 2

Systemic barriers to mental health treatment: Understanding where you stand

Many families and caregivers are unaware of the legal implications involved in securing treatment for a loved one of age. Involuntary commitment is often needed in severe cases, but difficult to get. It is the process by which families or others contact a healthcare facility to have someone treated without their consent. State and hospital policies deal with these requests differently, but most healthcare facilities will not utilize involuntary commitment without proof of imminent danger and due to HIPAA (Health Insurance Portability and Accountability Act), fails to include the family in the process. In the state of Pennsylvania and many others, 14-year-olds (or older) have the right to refuse treatment including medication. They also have the right to keep all things private. There are several problems in most states involving age and civil rights.

Age of consent

Adolescents are typically not mature enough to make decisions regarding multiple issues in their young lives. The mental health system is very complicated for adults with years of life experience, much less developing adolescents. It is difficult to understand why states entrust youngsters with legal authority regarding treatment when, for example, youths cannot consume alcohol until age 21. It makes greater sense to me that restrictions be placed on laws that allow kids to make treatment decisions if restrictions are placed on alcohol usage. Alcohol alters behavior and places the youth in danger almost as much as a severe or untreated mental health problem. Under age alcohol consumption and untreated or severe mental illness can seem to be one in the same. Therefore, legally they should be treated almost similarly. There are even age restrictions for when a youth can drive. Why aren't there restrictions for when adolescents can make treatment decisions when about 50% of mental health cases begin at age 14? Why aren't there restrictions when we know that 50% of 14-year-old students, according to the National Alliance for Mental Illness, drop out of high school due to mental health problems? These questions are for your state legislature and an issue to be brought before advocacy groups.

Civil commitment

An individual's age in addition to current civil commitment laws can be a real nightmare for families. When families recognize the need for treatment for their loved one, civil commitment laws make it ten times more difficult to secure treatment. It is also difficult for families to know what happens in treatment without consent. Families face two dilemmas: staying informed about treatment when an individual is of legal age and assisting their loved one in getting treatment when they cannot make the appropriate decision for themselves.

Most people who are suffering from a severe or untreated psychiatric disorder often struggle with perceptions of themselves and the world around them. This reality creates the condition necessary for more strict civil commitment laws. When an illness becomes so severe that an individual cannot decipher truth from fiction, reality from fantasy, or cannot keep themselves safe it is necessary for family members, caregivers, or friends to step in. For example, an individual suffering from paranoid schizophrenia may perceive that he is being watched by the government, becomes depressed, and refuses to leave his home. This behavior including isolation can lead to suicidal or homicidal thoughts. Most families then seek involuntary commitment. When that doesn't work, families seek to change the system. Consequently, in many states, this common sense action is met with resistance by bureaucrats, extreme anti-stigma supporters, and liberal law makers. A case close to home provides an example of this dilemma. A case in a Pennsylvania suburb, Richland Township involved a 26-year-old, Levi Staver, who fatally stabbed his grandmother in the back while she ate breakfast in her home in February of 2013. He reportedly explained to law enforcement that his grandmother was a witch and that he was commanded, by an archangel, to kill her. In the fall of 2012, Staver was diagnosed with schizophrenia. Years before this diagnosis, however, Staver's mother and grandparents attempted on multiple occasions to secure psychiatric treatment to no avail. The dilemma included his age, inability to recognize his need for treatment, and Pennsylvania's poorly designed civil commitment law.

There are multiple arguments against civil commitment. The first argument entails resistance to possible:

○ Decrease in civil liberties and autonomy

- o Increased familial involvement without permission
- o Over involvement of state decision making
- o Lack of patient input
- o Stigma
- o Fear of hospital policies returning to those of the 1700s

Typical arguments in favor of change to current civil commitment laws include:

- o Families need a certain level of control over obtaining treatment for their loved ones who are incapable of helping themselves.

- o Mental health professionals must protect society from potentially dangerous individual

- o Society must protect individuals who are not necessarily "dangerous" or "lethal" to self or others, but who still requires treatment.

- o We need a change in treatment laws in order to provide treatment to individuals who are unable to care for themselves and end up homeless, incarcerated, victimization, and violence.

Let's take a closer look at the many issues involving civil commitment and other laws in healthcare settings in the next section.

Historic and Contemporary Issues of civil commitment

Civil commitment is a legal process by which an individual with a mental illness can be voluntarily or involuntarily committed to a hospital for treatment. Arguments against the process of enhancing involuntary commitment laws dates back to the mid-1950s when civil rights attorneys, states, hospital staff, and advocates fought to reduce inpatient care. The detrimental consequences of this argument are noticeable in the increase in homelessness, victimization, crime, incarceration, and suicide. Enhanced civil commitment laws aim for stabilization and protection of the person and others. But some promoters of civil rights aim to influence families to believe independence will be reduced with changes to involuntary commitment laws. The opposite is actually the truth. Freedom will be enhanced because those with severe mental illnesses will not end up incarcerated, victimized, or engaging in an act of violence that leads to great consequences.

What most people fail to acknowledge is that stability of an individual with a severe or untreated mental illness is possible, but only with the right treatment combinations. Sadly, the majority of society closes their ears and minds to this truth. A balanced argument is rarely engaged in. The argument against better civil commitment laws has become more of a civil rights debate based on the preference of the majority and support of the 1st Amendment, rather than a debate of the best interest of needy patients, widespread lack of treatment, and facts. Supporters of current civil commitment laws are often individuals who do not believe they are ill, are civil rights attorneys, strong anti-stigma supporters, or individuals in "remission" and favoring the normalization of severe or untreated mental illness. The greatest concern amongst these individuals is that updates to civil commitment laws may make it less difficult for families and caregivers to request involuntary commitment for a loved one they are concerned about. Some critics fear for their own rights and freedom. Anyone with an open mind can see that supporters of changed civil commitment laws are trying to increase options, not decrease freedoms. Political forces still predominate. Previously, families could contact a magistrate and verbalize their concern in order to begin the process of involuntary commitment. Today, this flexibility is a thing of the past. Families are challenged to prove their loved one is a danger to self or others. Individuals of age must also verbalize a desire to harm self or others before commitment is considered. States make it almost impossible for individuals to be protected from their own illness. In an attempt to offer more independence and reduce stigma, policies have undermined the needs of those unable to care for themselves. The longest an individual can be held against their will in a psychiatric setting is 72 hours without a petition for longer stay. This is not usually enough time to stabilize individuals. Individuals are usually stabilized using medication and therapy and then released after 72 hours with brochures or referrals to outpatient clinics. Once the individual is released, they assume they are well enough to avoid further treatment or stop adhering to their medication schedule. The individual stops taking medication, attending therapy, or refuses to seek further treatment before ending up sick again. The individual may end up in another psychiatric setting against their will, incarcerated, or homeless. According to the Treatment Advocacy Center (2013), a center founded by Psychiatrist E. Fuller Torrey, between "150,000 and 200,000 individuals are homeless" due to lack of treatment. You would think these numbers would change things, but they haven't. As a beginning therapist in a Community Center working with

adults, I counseled a homeless female who not only refused
treatment but shelter. Her schizophrenia and substance abuse
blinded her to her own severe needs. She slept in her car and
refused to seek shelter. No therapist could help her, neither
could the law. Consider a similar story:

A young but homeless and mentally ill man, 37-year-old Kelly
Thomas, was fatally beaten to death by members of law
enforcement from the Fullerton Police Department in
California. Reports claim that his remains were
unrecognizable due to the fatal beating. Thomas was
suffering from schizophrenia and living on the streets. After
repeated back and forth orders from the police to Thomas,
excessive use of force and manslaughter resulted. In 2011,
both officers responsible for the initiation of the event were
charged (former Police Officer Manuel Ramos was charged
with second degree murder and involuntary manslaughter,
while former Corporal Police Officer Jay Cicinelli was
charged with involuntary manslaughter and use of excessive
force). If you would like to read more about this case and
other tragedies, visit the Treatment Advocacy Center's
Preventable Tragedies page:

www.treatmentadvocacycenter.org/problem/preventable-
tragedies-database.

"Dangerousness" criteria for involuntary commitment

Just read the daily news and it becomes apparent that our
laws are broken, incomprehensible, and haphazardly
designed. Washington D.C. enacted laws in 1964 to institute

the "dangerousness" standard that would require an individual meet certain criteria established by the state before being involuntarily committed. Most states adopted the "dangerousness" criteria in order to promote short-term, community based treatment over inpatient care. Testa and West (2012) state that a person must be:

> "determined to have a mental illness before he or she could be hospitalized against his or her will. Second, the person had to pose an imminent threat to the safety of him or herself or others or be shown to be "gravely disabled," meaning that he or she could not provide for the necessities for basic survival" (p.33).

They go on to state that "the district did not define the terms of the statue concretely, leaving some room for interpretation." (p.33). Many hospitals and agencies use this room for interpretation to decide what is critical and what is not. This has led to preventable tragedies nationwide. "Dangerousness" basically means that an individual has to have a detailed suicide or homicide plan to cause harm to self or others. "Imminent danger" usually refers to actions an individual will take (e.g., suicidal or homicidal) in the near future, primarily within 30 days. This criteria is too narrow to correctly identify those who may not be suicidal or homicidal but are, for example, actively psychotic and putting others in danger.

Current civil commitment laws can make it extremely difficult to have a loved one hospitalized involuntarily (known as a 302) even if families and caregivers express great concern and an individual appears very sick or has a history of threatening behavior. State laws require that an individual meet the "dangerousness" or "imminent danger" criteria or have an extensive plan to harm self or others before involuntary hospitalization can occur. In the state of Pennsylvania, "dangerousness" is characterized by:

o a "clear and present danger" (with a plan) to self or others. "Danger" specifically includes the inability, without assistance, to satisfy need for nourishment, personal or medical care, shelter, and self-protection or safety.
o a reasonable probability that death, serious bodily injury or serious physical debilitation will ensue within 30 days without treatment.

Many states have similar requirements for hospitalization. The dangerousness criteria was said to have first been adopted by the District of Columbia in 1964 and then by California, the most popular trend setting state (Anfang & Appelbaum, 2006). Other influences included court cases such as *O'Connor vs. Donaldson* in 1975 and *Lessard vs. Schmidt* in 1976. Both cases ruled it unconstitutional to confine someone capable of caring for their basic needs. States followed these trend setters. As a result, resources are now being invested in multiple community mental health services. While well-meaning, constant promotion of these community programs draw attention away from the most vulnerable. For example, Pennsylvania has become a mobile therapy-based, community mental health supporter. It has not only closed its Harrisburg state hospital, but also implemented more programs in Community Treatment Teams (CTT). CTT provides assertive treatment within the community. Pennsylvania is well known for its CASSP program (Children and Adolescent Service System Program), which also provides community-based programs. Most therapist jobs in

Pennsylvania are mobile or in-home based. While it is important to help individuals maintain themselves within their community (if their illness is stabilized), we cannot overlook the dire needs of those who are unstable within our communities such as those with untreated severe illnesses. Our modern civil commitment laws are too black and white. Do we have to wait until a tragedy occurs to receive treatment? We should not, but we often do. Mental illness is very complex and includes a lot of gray areas. As a result of this black and white perspective, society has had to (and will continue to) pay a great price for systemic barriers to treatment, poor civil commitment laws, and strong support of short-term treatment. The beginning of this nightmare dates back to the early 1950s with de-institutionalization.

Pre and post de-Institutionalization

Because of the historical abuse and abandonment of the homeless, severely ill, and vulnerable psychiatric patients in the United States, many who oppose changing involuntary commitment laws are resisting a return to such treatment. Testa and West (2010) state that:

> "Prior to the inception of American asylums, people with mental illness were relegated to prisons and shelters for the poor. In these settings, the distinction between voluntary and involuntary admissions to psychiatric hospitals [were not clear]; all admissions were involuntary. Furthermore, because many institutions operated on private funding, it was quite possible for families to purchase the confinement of unwanted relatives" (p. 32).

WHAT EVERY PARENT, FAMILY MEMBER, & CAREGIVER SHOULD KNOW

This horrific past has sadly engrained itself into the minds of anti-stigma citizens. It has painted the perception of involuntary psychiatric commitment incorrectly. It is important that hospital policymakers and citizens understand that mental health treatment will not return to the barbaric treatment of the mentally ill in the early 1200s. With proper monitoring of the system, education, and awareness, we are likely to go forward, not backward. But some still don't believe this is possible and remain influenced by their knowledge of historic accounts of treating the mentally ill. During the mid-1200s, patients were automatically presumed to be incapable of making appropriate treatment decisions, even if this was not the case. All admissions were involuntary, no one had a say. The state acted as what is known as parens patriae (Latin for "father of his country"), a doctrine that grants power to a government to act in the manner of a "parent" for individuals incapable of helping themselves (e.g., the mentally ill or children). The mental health field sought to change this "state power" over time.

In the modernity of our times, involuntary treatment is not legally permitted unless an individual is severe enough (dangerous to self or others) to be committed to a psychiatric facility. This standard is likely to remain firm, even if involuntary commitment laws change. The problematic reality is that our current system for involuntary commitment is based on poorly established criteria that offers no flexibility in severe cases. The criteria caters to those who know how to "play the system." Many patients have become familiar with the system and often refuse to relinquish any details of a suicide or homicide plan to a healthcare provider for fear of being "apprehended." Therefore, many patients learn to "play the game" or "keep a low profile" while receiving treatment. Healthcare providers remain oblivious to behaviors or treatment needs that can eventually lead to a tragedy. Mental health professionals are never completely able to predict an individual's behavior. Many tragedies result from this poorly constructed system of psychiatric care.

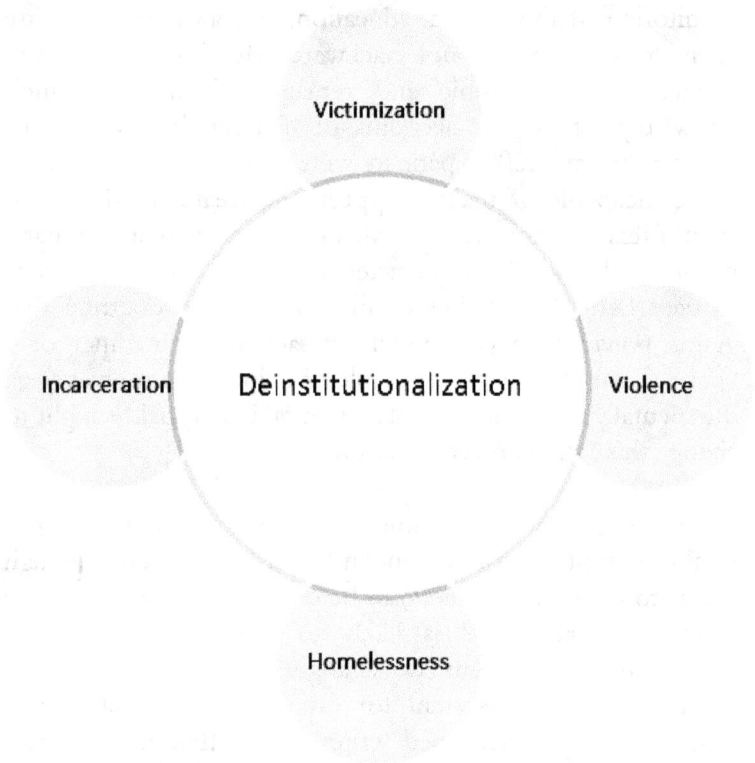

Victimization

Incarceration   Deinstitutionalization   Violence

Homelessness

Image 1: De-institutionalization is at the center of some of our major systemic problems such as victimization, homelessness, incarceration, and violence.

De-institutionalization, the process of reducing long-term care, has created much controversy. As a result of this exodus movement, many leading professionals in the field of psychiatry claim that the result has not been positive. In fact, we currently have high rates of incarceration (i.e., criminalization of the mentally ill), homelessness, victimization, and violence (see figure 2-11) (Torrey, 2008). Families, caregivers, and friends hate to discuss the negativity associated with mental illness, lack of treatment available, and the aloneness that accompanies the sick and their loved ones. Various movements have resulted from this fear of discussion and the most prominent today is the "anti-stigma" and civil rights movements:

Anti-stigma

Individuals of the anti-stigma campaigns often focus on removing negatives associated with mental illness and seeking treatment. The goal is to normalize the experience of families, friends, caretakers, and individual sufferers. Some anti-stigma supporters refuse to use the term "mental illness" but would rather use the term "mental disorder" or "mental disease." The goal of most anti-stigma supporters is to get rid of or reduce the need for hospitalization, even to the extent of downplaying what they know is significantly needed to treat severe illness. Severe mental illness is a "small" portion of the population to some anti-stigma supporters.

Civil Rights

Most supporters of civil rights in mental health are often radically in favor of outpatient treatment. They do not like to focus on severe mental illness and they almost completely despise involuntary commitment. Supporters believe it is against the civil rights of individuals to be hospitalized against one's will. This view has become very problematic within the mental health system because it's too narrow. Many civil rights supporters lack a balanced perspective and simply do not want involuntary commitment laws to be adjusted.

The foundation of the anti-stigma and civil rights movements can ultimately pose great challenges to families and caregivers seeking treatment, especially in cases of severe mental illness.

The exodus of patients during the mid-1960s to the early 1970s (known today as de-institutionalization) has led to the removal of severely mentally ill or under-treated individuals from state hospitals and into society where incarceration, violence, victimization, and homelessness became a frequent reality. Sadly, many discharged patients were not given referrals or follow-up meetings to monitor progress within the community. While this movement was intended to provide autonomy, it led to chaos, lack of treatment, and little to no aftercare. There are two historically important and problematic issues that families are unformed about which includes: modification of the mental health system through civil rights movements and the introduction of psychiatric medication. Both of these incidents contributed to the views on short-term care.

Modification of the system

The support of de-institutionalization was influenced by many, but mainly the advocacy of two lawyers: Bruce Ennis and Thomas Zander. Ennis, who died in 2000, was a 1st Amendment "expert" and national legal Director of the American Civil Liberties Union. He spent several years directing the Mental Health Law Project, which focused on fighting for the constitutional rights of hospitalized mental health patients. It is important that we understand the deep issues inherent in mental health care before we start advocating change, which is something Ennis failed to consider. As Dr. E. Fuller Torrey, MD (2008) quoted in his book, *The insanity offense: How America's failure to treat the seriously mentally ill endangers its citizens*, "Ennis's avowed goal was nothing less than the abolition of involuntary hospitalization and the ultimate closure of all mental hospitals." Torrey believes that de-institutionalization is one component that has contributed to the majority of the homeless, incarcerated, victimized, and dangerous in our society today. I am of the firm belief that outmoded laws have led to reduced access to proper care and negative consequences in our communities such as:

o poorly enforced treatment options
o lack of family involvement in decision making where appropriate
o short stays in psychiatric hospitals
o difficulty with involuntary commitment in severe but not lethal cases

The biggest barrier I have witnessed in families is having to prove a loved one needs treatment, even though the individual may not be lethal. For example, a mother who has a son with severe bipolar disorder and abusing substances could not be committed to a psychiatric hospital unless he was a danger to himself or others. He must be on the brink of death before he could be committed. The only way he could be committed is if he signed himself into the hospital, a very unlikely circumstance.

Introduction of psychiatric medication

Due to the much anticipated introduction of psychotropic drugs, de-institutionalization appeared genius. This was the beginning of tragedy for many. The introduction of anti-psychotics such as Lithium or Haldol contained severe symptoms and allowed most to live independently with reduced chaos. Meds helped support the view that inpatient care could become a last resort choice. As a result, many states pursued ways to reduce long-term care. But strict legal criteria for being committed has created more barriers rather than freedom. Let's face it, there are times when commitment is appropriate to protect the individual and others. While some individuals may be able to maintain themselves safely within the community, many are not. How do we treat them? We cannot overlook them because we decide stigma is too powerful to battle or because we decide normalization of severe or untreated mental illness is a better way to go. We have to face the facts and the facts say that we have neglected the treat the sickest of the sick.

As a supporter of outpatient and less restrictive care, I encourage you to consider options that best suits your situation. But I also encourage families to seek inpatient care, residential care, and hospitalization if strict monitoring is needed. To reduce negative consequences, inpatient care is often needed for people likely to end up in bad scenarios. The purpose of hospitalization is stabilization, not imprisonment. Once we open our mind to the full purpose of involuntary commitment and assisted outpatient treatment (discussed in chapter 4), we can possibly offer the flexibility that families and caretakers of the severely ill desire.

Confidentiality & HIPAA: Barriers to treatment

Great controversy has arisen over the years regarding the rigid restrictions of confidentiality and HIPAA. Parents, spouses, caregivers, and healthcare providers all have had difficulty with the protective rules of both HIPAA and confidentiality. HIPAA, the Health Insurance Portability and Accountability Act of 1996, protects medical and mental health information from being exposed to the public or others who do not have permission to access a patient file. It also controls how information about a patient can be shared with others. There are two important rules: 1.) Privacy Rule (which gives patients certain rights and provides federal protections) and 2.) Security Rule (which requires covered entities or healthcare facilities to take certain safeguards in the sharing of patient files). Faxes, emails, paper forms, and other correspondences within or outside of a medical or mental health agency must be handled with care. If your loved one has been hospitalized or cared for in a healthcare setting, their information is protected under HIPAA's Privacy and Security Rule. It is difficult to retrieve information regarding the diagnosis, treatment plan, or medication treatment on a loved one, despite proof of your association with the individual (e.g., daughter/son, wife/husband, or parent). In order to receive what is known as Protected Health Information (PHI) on another individual, HIPAA requires the patient to complete what is known as an authorization to release information form. This form requires a signature (or sometimes a verbal approval) from the patient to allow another person access to records. If an "outsider" (family member, caregiver, friend, or healthcare provider) is not documented as a personal representative, Power of Attorney or guardian, or the patient did not sign a release of information form, PHI will be very difficult if not impossible to retrieve (even in emergencies). Each state, however, is different. So you want to understand your state law when it comes to HIPAA Privacy and Security Rules.

If your loved one is interested in reviewing psychotherapy notes, information compiled for legal proceedings, or medical records from correctional centers, it may be difficult to obtain them. Any healthcare provider can refuse to allow full access to records, even though HIPAA's Privacy Rule states that a patient has the right to review and obtain a copy of their PHI. The reality is that if a healthcare provider believes access to records can be "harmful" to a patient, they can prevent access to part or all of that record. In many cases, some organizations do not have to abide by HIPAA's rules and regulations such as law enforcement agencies, most schools or school districts, municipal offices, workers compensation carriers, employers, or life insurers. However, covered entities (which are often healthcare facilities) must abide by HIPAA's rules the majority of the time. But you must be aware that there are exceptions which include: a public health emergency, serious threat, bio-terrorism, court order or subpoena, suspense of child abuse or neglect, and a psychotherapists discretion. Unfortunately, many patients do not have as much control as they would like to have because HIPAA ultimately controls access to records. As a result, the biggest problem involving mental healthcare are found amongst those families experiencing hurdles resulting from regulations. For these reasons, I recommend all families carefully read the Notice of Privacy Practices. You can request this from a healthcare provider if it is not given to you upon your initial visit.

Visit the U.S. Department of Health and Human Services for further information on HIPAA (see suggested resources). To download a copy of the Notice of Privacy Practices, visit http://www.hhs.gov/ocr/privacy/hipaa/understanding/cove redentities/notice.html. HIPAA has also created multiple problems for healthcare providers in retrieving health records for coordination of care. For example, if your loved one is receiving care from a neurologist and his psychiatrist needs records before psychiatric treatment can begin, the psychiatrist will request that your loved one complete an authorization to release information form. These forms are also sometimes called release of information forms. For youngsters under age 14, parents will grant permission for review or transfer of health records.

Confidentiality

Confidentiality is defined as your legal and moral right to privacy in a healthcare setting. Confidentiality is another hurdle to treatment and creates great difficulty for families who desire to know what the progress of their loved one is (discussed further in next section). A mental health therapist has ethical obligations to abide by when providing treatment protecting their privacy. As a result, therapists only provide necessary information, when appropriate, to "outsiders." A therapist or healthcare provider will never breach confidentiality without a clear reason. Even if patient information is shared with "outsiders," only the necessary information to accomplish a goal will be shared. For example, therapists have ethical duties to carry out in a therapeutic relationship and if a therapist determines it necessary to abide by these duties, "outsiders" will only receive necessary information regarding the patient. Otherwise, all healthcare information is kept confidential. Here is a list of major duties of a therapist:

- o Duty to warn: This standard refers to the therapist's duty to protect other people who are possibly in danger at the hands of the person receiving mental health care. For example, if a client states that he is very angry with his wife, has a PFA order, and verbalizes his desire to kill his wife, a therapist has a legal duty to warn her. Failing to warn the wife can result in major legal and ethical consequences.
- o Duty to report: Therapists are required by law to report incidents of potential abuse (sexual, physical, emotional) in the event it is strongly suspected. Most healthcare providers are mandated reporters.

o "Duty to comply": If required by a court-order to provide information in a case regarding an individual's mental health records, a therapist must release information.

A therapist also has an obligation to protect the information shared in a therapy session from the public (even family members or spouses). In the event an individual in therapy is perceived as needing serious intervention, there are three exceptions to breaking confidentiality:

o If an individual threatens to harm someone else
o If an individual threatens to harm him/herself
o If an individual reports that he/she has been abused

Therapists use their discretion in also reporting promiscuous behaviors of adolescents, extreme drug and alcohol abuse, or other risky behaviors.

Children & Adolescents In Treatment

In cases where a child or adolescent may be in individual or group therapy they have a right to confidentiality. Confidentiality says that "I will not share anything you share with me, as your therapist or healthcare provider, outside of this office." It offers youth an opportunity to share personal details without the fear of parents ever finding out about what was discussed. In many cases, therapists will not reveal sensitive details of a session unless a child:

o Threatens to kill or seriously harm him/herself
o Threatens to kill or seriously harm someone else

o   Reports abuse

Again, a therapist will use their discretion in reporting incidents such as chronic substance abuse or promiscuity. However, in many cases, that child or adolescent is legally entitled to confidentiality. State laws and counseling centers vary when it comes to reporting details of a counseling session involving children and adolescents. Most cases will require that a therapist utilize their intuition, discernment, and previous experiences to determine appropriate ways to report or share certain details. For younger children (ages 5-13), retrieving information about a counseling session or treatment in general will be a tad easier. The older the child gets, the harder it will be to determine what is going on in regards to treatment.

Parents, caregivers, and families will have some rights when it comes to caring for the mental health of a young family member. But if a 14-year-old, in some states, does not believe they need treatment, they can refuse it and become noncompliant. The most a therapist can legally do is try to encourage and motivate a youngster to give treatment a try. Most kids are unsure of what to expect and fear entering treatment. Some therapists are really good at dissuading the negative perceptions. Some therapists are also good at making therapy fun for kids and educational. In most cases all a child needs is support and knowledge about therapy in order to accept it. Nevertheless, I often encourage parents and families to maintain open communication with their youngers regarding treatment. Open communication will help kids speak more readily about therapy sessions and treatment in general. Your goal is to remain in the loop about treatment as much as possible.

Adults In Treatment

Many families end up realizing the little legal control they have over the mental health treatment of a loved one who is at legal age. This is why I recommend that ALL families seek what are known as Mental Health Advanced Directives, Power of Attorneys, or personal representatives (individuals who can legally make decisions for a patient). A mental health advanced directive is basically a "living will." It allows the individual with a severe or untreated mental illness to sign rights over to a trusted individual who can make healthcare decisions on their behalf. The living will document is quite long but doesn't require an attorney, legal advice, or complicated information. You can complete a mental health advanced directive form in the company of your case manager, therapist, or a notary.

A power of attorney is someone your loved one has designated, in writing, to make significant decisions involving mental health care when they are unable to do so themselves. One hundred percent of control goes to the designee (person who has been designated the power of attorney).

The person completing an advanced directives or power of attorney form will be guided through a series of questions regarding:

- o How they would like to receive treatment in the event they are unable to verbalize their preferences
- o Where they would like to be taken in case of an emergency
- o Who they would prefer to speak on their behalf if they cannot speak to anyone

o   Whether they want to receive medication or not
o   What medical conditions they may have that could interfere with medication use

If you feel safer seeking legal advice, I encourage you to do so. The main purpose of these forms is to document who will take care of the person who may become too impaired to make important decisions. In the state of Pennsylvania you can find psychiatric advanced directives and power of attorney forms at the Mental Health Association (see suggested resources). In all other states, you can contact your local Health Department and inquire, contact your local NAMI organization for direction, or visit the National Resource Center on Advanced Directives (see suggested resources). Ultimately, the goal is to stay informed, know what your rights are, and document your loved one's wishes. In the next section we will review some relevant questions you need to ask if your loved one is hospitalized.

When your loved one needs to be hospitalized

Many families and caregivers cringe at the thought of having to seek involuntary commitment for a loved one who is of age. The fear of not knowing what to expect, what to say, or what to do can encourage a host of negative emotions that are just as crippling as your loved ones mental distress. But there are questions families and caregivers can arm themselves with before, during, and after hospitalization to lighten the load. When your loved one needs hospitalization (voluntarily or involuntarily) there are many questions that flow through the mind. As you or your loved one sign thousands of forms and ask the questions that overwhelm your mind, you wonder if you are doing all the right things, signing the right forms, or asking the right questions. When it's time to leave, you walk away, feeling unsure about the whole thing and wondering what the next step is. Many feel guilty and others fear they will be hated by the individual for being hospitalized or by others who disagree with the hospitalization itself. It will be important to separate how angry your loved one may be with you from their severe need of treatment. Thankfully, there are things you can do to make the process of a hospitalization less of a nightmare. Below you will find a brief list of "starter" questions to ask that will aid you in the process of voluntary or involuntary hospitalization. I'm sure you would rather not deal with hospitalization, but when and if you do, you need to be armed with the correct questions to ask.

Questions to ask before, during, & after hospitalization

Before hospitalization

o Is hospitalization absolutely necessary or are there other options I can consider?
o Will my loved one receive a psychiatric evaluation? How long will it be? Can I accompany him/her?
o How long will he/she be here?
o What type of clothes can he/she wear and can I bring my own?
o Do I need to bring basic care supplies (brush, comb, tooth brush, etc.)?
o Will he/she be allowed to receive phone calls?

During hospitalization

Medication

o What are the doctor's recommendations?
o Will my loved one be forced to take medication?
o What would justify being medicated against one's will in this setting?
o Is my loved one currently on any medications?
o Can I receive a print out or list of medications prescribed?
o Can someone speak to me about potential side effects?

Questions for children and adolescents

- What can I do about my child/adolescent missing school?
- Can I have the hospital write a note to the school to make up for absences?
- Can my child/adolescent bring books, electronic devices, or activities?

Financial

- When will billing occur?
- What type of insurance do you take?
- What can I do if I don't have insurance
- Are there payment plans available?
- Are there local federal and state programs that can help me get insurance?

After hospitalization and discharge

Continual Treatment

- Can I petition for my loved one to stay longer if I feel this is needed?
- Can I have a referral to outpatient treatment centers?
- Do you have a list of referrals to therapists in our area?
- Where could I possibly find a listing of local mental health support groups?

o   If I need to petition the courts for assisted treatment, who can I talk to about this? (Note: make sure your state supports assisted outpatient treatment first).

It is always useful if families know what to expect, what to say, and what to question in psychiatric settings. Try not to feel intimidated by your loved one's healthcare provider so much that you are unable to get all of your questions answered and concerns taken seriously. Of course, you do not want to overwhelm staff who are already inundated. However, you do want to make sure that you develop a sound relationship with your loved one's healthcare provider so that you can ask questions and share concerns. As discussed in chapter 1, you want to pursue providers who make you feel understood, have a balanced perspective, has an open-mind, and who can offer your loved one the type of treatment and personal care you know they deserve.

Conclusion

While looking at the multiplicity of systemic barriers (civil commitment, de-institutionalization or short-term treatment, age of consent laws, confidentiality, and HIPAA), it becomes apparent that the system of mental health is replete with high levels of stress, controversy, politics, resistance to change, and even fear. The reason why so many people resist changing current treatment laws is usually due to fear of stigma. While it is very important to reduce stigma, we are ultimately self-destructing. The hard reality is that criminalization of the mentally ill (imprisoning people who need help), victimization, homicide (resulting in 1,600 homicides per year), and homelessness (between 150,000 and 200,000 individuals) greet families more regularly than we care to admit. Stigma creates barriers to treatment because people are afraid of seeking help due to discrimination. But people are also not being treated appropriately because the proper treatment options do not exist. As a result, we have two problems that we are battling incorrectly. Instead of reducing the perception of severe mental illness and trying to reduce stigma, we should be changing laws, providing more resources, and educating the public. The time to act is way overdue. It is important that we, who understand the issues that prevent proper and timely treatment, weigh the pros and cons of promoting more flexible commitment laws and become active to make change happen. Conversation is extremely important, but change without action is a distant dream.

Chapter 3

The so-called "bible" of diagnoses: A history everyone should know about

$\mathcal{T}$he field of mental health underwent major transformations between the early 1950s and 1970s including multiple developments and revisions of the Diagnostic and Statistical Manual of Mental Disorders (DSM). Changes also occurred in civil commitment laws, how much control families had in the care of loved ones, and the use of psychotropic medications. Most of the transformations that occurred during this time, primarily involving civil commitment, were not due to advances in knowledge about mental health, but rather changing social, political, and cultural ideologies. According to Anfang and Appelbaum (2006), "American civil commitment law has reflected the swinging pendulum of social attitudes towards civil commitment, oscillating between more and less restriction…"(p.209). The DSM was originally created to provide a common language between professionals regarding symptoms and concerns presented to clinicians. Before the development and publication of the DSM-I in the early 1950s, various systems were created and used to describe mental health and behavior in clinical settings. During this time, little was known about mental illness and behavior. The field was just beginning to discuss ways to better understand mental illness, ways to improve treatment and access, and short term care for mental health problems. Psychotropic drugs, new discoveries, and new labels were all entering the field and quite frankly, confusing everyone. As discussed in chapter 2, these so-called "advances" in the field created systemic barriers that currently prevent timely and appropriate mental health services for the severely ill. Not only is de-institutionalization and poor aftercare to blame, but so too is under-diagnosis (leading to untreated mental illness) and over-diagnosis (leading to wasted time on a diagnosis that isn't the real problem).

The development of the DSM & political influence

The DSM, although widely accepted and authoritative in multiple fields, is one of the most political documents in existence. Its development and subsequent revisions have led to a storm of controversy and arguments over what should be included and excluded and what should be defined as a "mental disorder." No one can agree on how to define mental illness because symptoms within a disorder vary and people suffering from two separate disorders can look quite identical, making differentiation difficult and increasing misdiagnosis. Researchers and so-called "scientists" are blinded by labels, titles, and prestige. So the DSM is far from a scientifically supported document. It has been defined and re-defined over time to reflect the "majority rule" and the desires, cultural changes, and social ideologies of our society. For example, the DSM was created in the early 1920s and based on Freudian ideology, a plethora of unstable banter representative of psychoanalytic psychology that resulted in unfounded diagnoses and erroneous assumptions about parenting, women, and mental health in general (Citizens Commission On Human Rights International, 2011). Much controversy surrounds the document's revisions and many questioning individuals wonder if mental illness is actually on the increase or if multiple revisions are making it much easier to categorize "normal" expressions of human behavior as "abnormal." Whether this is true or not true remains to be seen. But this does not erase the deficits of the manual. The Citizens Commission on Human Rights International (2011), a self-proclaimed nonpolitical, nonreligious, and nonprofit mental health "watchdog," claims that:

"...One could argue that each change in the DSM has essentially recruited a new batch of subjects for identification and treatment.....The new DSM is coming, probably in 2013 or 2014 — a lot later than its original projected deadline of 2011, in part because debates over what it should include have been so fierce.... [T]he more important critique is that the fundamental underpinnings of the DSM are flawed, and that the lack of a theoretical basis means that any quirk or problem a person might express can be categorized as illness. Even expert tautological logic is still tautological."

In the development of the DSM-V, questions arose about what actually is a mental illness and so-called disorders were changed to reflect modern views of mental health. Much of the information discussed during the making of the DSM-V superseded our actual knowledge base. Former Chair of the DSM-IV Task Force states that "the DSM had become too powerful for its own good and society's." He goes on to express that:

"the new disorders prompted so blithely by my friends would create tens of millions of new 'patients.' I pictured all these normal enough people being captured in the DSM-5's excessively wide diagnostic net, and worried that many would be exposed to unnecessary medicine with possibly dangerous side effects" (p.14)

Each change in the DSM has expressed society's standards and desire to conform to new social, cultural, and political beliefs about mental illness. During the early 1950s the DSM consisted of only 108 diagnostic categories. But sixteen years after the publication of the DSM-I, the DSM-II was created and included about 182 new diagnostic categories (Pomeroy & Parrish, 2012). During the early 1970s, the DSM was

overhauled by the strict political and cultural desires of the
people (the majority rule). For example, in the 1970s multiple
gay rights riots erupted after the sexual liberation movement
and the violent stonewall riots of the 60s. Protests were
aimed at the American Psychiatric Association (the author of
the DSM) after the inclusion of homosexuality in the DSM-II
as a mental illness (Pomeroy & Parrish, 2012). In 1974, after
great political pressure to sink its empire, the American
Psychiatric Association voted to remove homosexuality from
the DSM-II. This vote was not based on a scientific
foundation, but rather social, cultural, and political pressure.
This manner of political control has led to multiple text
revisions (TR) and confusion over the exact definition and
nature of mental illness. For centuries, professionals have
been arguing over what constitutes a mental illness and what
constitutes normal behavior. At this point in the game, almost
everything is a mental illness requiring treatment (medication
and therapy). Although mental illness, behavioral, and
developmental disorders exists at alarming rates today,
"researchers" have begun categorizing everything but the
kitchen sink as mentally ill. This embarrassment has resulted
in many leaving the mental health field, revolting it, or
dedicating themselves to changing it.

By the 1980s, the DSM-III included a total of 265 disorders and "an attempt was made to empirically validate the classification of mental disorders (Keely et al., 2008, as cited in Pomeroy & Parrish, 2012, p.196). Even with the DSM's shaky history and revisions (DSM-I in 1952, DSM-II in 1968, DSM-III in 1980, DSM-III-R in 1987, DSM-IV in 1994, DSM-IV-TR in 2000, and DSM-V in 2013), the field of psychiatry has come to regard the manual as a "bible," a book that includes everything professionals need to make a logical and intelligent diagnosis of symptomatology. Pomeroy and Parrish (2012) state that the DSM "is used not only by the medical profession, but also by the majority of mental health professionals, insurance companies, researchers, grant-funded agencies, and academicians in the United States for diagnostic, assessment, and educational purposes" (P.195). However, the lack of scientific rigor and research is what makes this book less than a "bible." For the sake of being politically correct, a bible is a canonical and factually inspired collection of works that results from an established doctrine by a Higher Authority, a Deity. The "higher authority" of the DSM is the cultural and social desire of human beings, people with faults and hidden agendas. In this sense, the DSM is nothing more than a 943+ page document that reflects the fantasy and dreams of "elite leading professionals" in the field who aim to change the perception of mental illness. Seeing their ideas in "lights" and feeling accomplished supersedes true healthcare. As Frances (2013) said about working on the DSM-IV, "I felt an exhilarating sense of power as I plotted possible ways to change and improve psychiatry" (p.13). Those experiencing this "power" are those pre-chosen based on status and reputation. This is not a fairly pre-chosen group of "scientists."

In the development of the DSM-V, the committees chosen to discuss changes for the DSM-IV-TR included a pre-chosen group of individuals (29 Task Force Members, 13 DSM Workgroups, 6 study groups to address issues relevant to all work groups) in addition to sponsorship from the biggest conglomerates in the mental health system (National Institute of Mental Health, the American Psychological Association, and American Psychiatric Association) (Pomeroy & Parrish, 2012). These "power-houses" are replete with opinions and influence public perception simply due to their position within the field. Pomeroy and Parrish (2012) stated that there was "strict criteria for membership" in the design of the DSM-V (p.197). This "strict criteria" creates a group of individuals who hold similar views for society and its changing culture. With the new DSM-V, it has become clear that the DSM is nothing more than a simple political caricature of professionalism that serves nothing greater than labels. The DSM-V, released in May 2013, has become a labeling machine. In fact, the DSM continues to lack scientific validity and is largely out of touch with reality. An in-depth evaluation of its origin often leads to shocking findings and disturbing evidence. Therapist and author, James Davis (2013) points to the medicalization of psychiatric health and believes the DSM to be the main tool by which psychiatry and pharmaceutical companies can change the view of mental illness. He believes that mental illness is over-diagnosed and over-medicated. Of course, many people in denial about mental illness often agree with this view. However, what Davis shares with us is still worth considering, but considering with caution. Director of the National Institute of Mental Health, Dr. Thomas R. Insel (2013), believes that psychiatry should now include research into biological causes and genetics, not symptoms themselves. He further states that the DSM does not reflect the "complexity of many disorders." He makes a basic point that "while [the] DSM has been described as a "Bible" for the field, it is, at best, a dictionary, creating a set of labels and defining each." He agrees that the DSM's validity is quite weak and has never reflected the truth. It's about time we understand the truth and reframe from becoming victims.

Many supporters of the DSM will adhere to its rules, utilize its diagnostic categories without questioning its benefit, site "research and statistical findings" they claim are concrete, and exclaim the DSM's intent to clarify outdated diagnostic categories. For example, the DSM-V will no longer include the personality disorder Narcissistic Personality Disorder. The explanation is quite vague, but supporters of the DSM-V claim that the removal of this diagnostic entity will catapult the field of psychiatry into a greater understanding of personality disorders. But many see this as a mistake because people who have characteristics of narcissism will not be "clinically" acknowledged. Nelson (2013) states that:

> "Without Narcissistic Personality Disorder in the DSM 5, there theoretically would be no such entity—no recognition, no treatment, no insurance reimbursement. To me, this would be a huge omission in medicine and psychiatry.... Dr. John Gunderson, who helped create the current DSM IV Manual has said, 'They have little appreciation for the damage they could be doing. It's draconian.' I agree." (p.295).

Similarly, the new diagnostic label for kids (ages 6-18 year old) who have 3+ temper tantrums a week, known as Disruptive Mood Dysregulation Disorder (DMDD), reduces the integrity of the field and those who plan on using this label in their clinical work. Through my eyes as I see it as a therapist, DMDD was approved in favor of presuming social and cultural theories on the over-diagnosis of bipolar disorder, not a greater understanding of mental health. Looking at the DSM from this angle helps us recognize more clearly the errors inherent in the DSM's construction and continual revisions. According to Pomeroy and Parrish (2012) "its development has consistently reflected the U.S. zeitgeist, including the relevant import of theory or research in guiding the conceptualization of mental illness, the definition of mental illness, and political and social developments within mainstream American culture" (p.195). Because we do not completely understand mental illness and human behavior, the way to cope with a nebulous problem is to change its meaning in a way that provides some understanding. This is what the DSM does. In doing this, we reduce the problem to fit our culturally and socially constructed minds, which ultimately creates greater problems because we lose sight of what truly is an illness and what truly isn't an illness.

The next section focuses on holistic health and the need to evaluate what the entire human body needs, not just the mind. When your loved one is diagnosed, it is important to inquire about nutrition or follow up with your medical doctor, asking for suggestions on how to create a holistic plan.

Embracing DSM diagnoses holistically

When seeking mental health treatment for your loved one, it is important to be open to holistic approaches to psychiatric care. Families should encourage a healthcare professional to give them a treatment plan that focuses on the entire being, not just the mental health aspect (see figure 3.2). For example, some psychiatrists and mental health therapists will utilize approaches to treatment that include exercise, better eating practices, vitamin intake, or a sleep schedule. When I work with children or adolescents and their families I often encourage them to watch for side effects and incorporate a sleeping schedule, better eating habits, and exercise regimen. Unfortunately, a lot of mental health professionals fail to pay attention to overall health and only consider it when concerns arise or medication and therapy aren't successful.

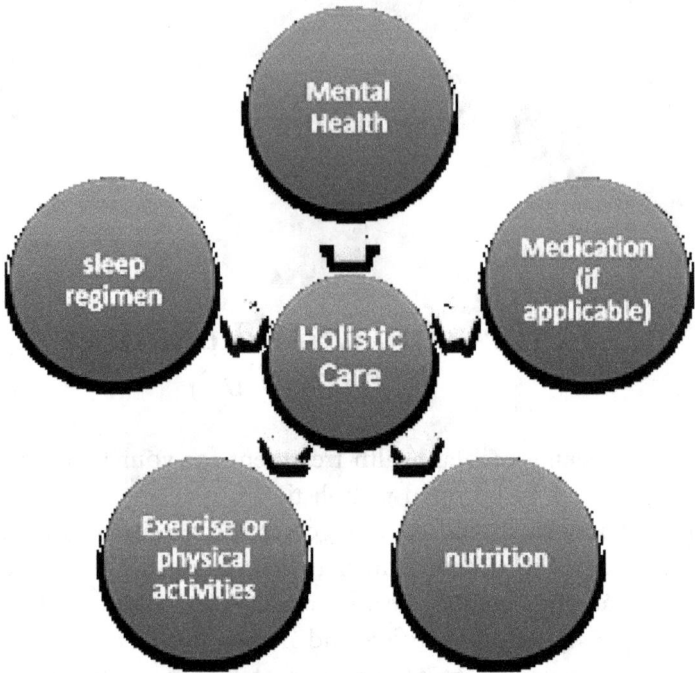

Image 2: Conceptualize care from a holistic perspective by looking at the entire human structure. Spiritual awareness is also just as important as the above.

When you develop a holistic perspective you also learn to keep an eye out for underlying medical causes to psychiatric symptoms. For example, many psychiatric diagnoses are mistaken for medical conditions and vice versa. According to a Wall Street Journal Health Journal report (2011), studies have shown that "medical conditions may cause mental health conditions in as many as 25% of psychiatric patients and contribute to them in more than 75%" of cases. A diagnosis of anxiety or depression is often misdiagnosed as "psychological" when depression and anxiety may in fact be related to your thyroid gland or anemia. This is a medical situation that requires medical attention and may not respond well to therapy alone. Even if your loved one has been diagnosed with a mental illness, keep in mind that you can still contribute to the overall improvement of the illness by eating right, exercising, and paying attention to overall health. In clinical settings, it is not common practice for a therapist or other mental health professional to consider medical conditions before diagnosing a mental illness. Unfortunately, therapists are trained to focus specifically on both the psychological and emotional components of a presenting concern, not the medical aspect. So individuals often receive a psychiatric diagnosis with a referral to seek medical or neurological assessment if a concern arises. The most a therapist will do is offer a referral, if requested, to other healthcare providers. It is often useful for families seeking psychiatric treatment to also get a second opinion if an assessment doesn't feel right. Misdiagnosis is more frequent than we'd like to believe. Falchuk (2009) discusses in his article how second opinions can actually save lives when treatment is being sought and how a misdiagnosis can greatly affect treatment:

> "As much as 30% of U.S. heath care costs are attributable to…misguided medical care. But behind these hundreds of billions of dollars in wasted expenditures, there is the human suffering that occurs when someone goes through the health care system without a clear path, or worse, the wrong path…." (p.26).

Falchuk (2009) goes on to state that many employees of medical establishments are mis-diagnosed:

> "These are heartbreaking situations where employees have faced difficult medical decisions and haven't known where to turn—situations where employees found out, sometimes too late, that there was another test they should have had, other treatments they should have pursued, other doctors they could have seen." (p.26).

Parents, families, and caregivers should strive to be open minded about diagnoses, provide as much information during assessments as you can (even if you think information is irrelevant), and pursue holistic avenues to treating a mental illness. The human body is complex and the brain is even more convoluted. If a particular medication isn't helping your loved one, mention it. If a particular treatment isn't effective, mention it. For me, holistic health includes working with the whole individual and finding out what combined treatments (e.g., medication and a sleep schedule or medication and dieting) can affect overall health. Similarly, be open to clinical recommendations no matter how difficult the diagnosis may be. Be wise with second opinions as well. While second opinions can be useful in getting appropriate and timely treatments, many healthcare settings will pull records from previous services used (becoming influenced by them) and may not yield different results. Second opinions cost money which can become astronomical. Even more, second opinions require patience, lots of tests, and time. Just be prepared to endure.

Conclusion

My criticisms of the Diagnostic and Statistical Manual of Mental Disorders are reviews of the issues that plague the field of psychiatry as well as families and caregivers across the nation. My criticisms, however, are not intended to reduce the partial usefulness of the manual. The DSM can be useful in situations where diagnostic interpretation of symptoms is complicated or where two or more diagnoses may be possible. In previous clinical work, I have used the DSM to help structure my understanding of what my clinical knowledge suggested might be the case with certain clients. The DSM can be useful to clinicians in aiding them in making a proper diagnosis or at least in approximating their diagnoses to what could be occurring within an individual. The biggest problem of all with the DSM is its political foundation. We get nowhere when we rely on politics and science takes a backseat. The goal of this chapter is to enlighten parents, families, and caregivers to important considerations and hidden arguments between professionals in the field of psychiatry and psychotherapy. With a greater understanding of the arguments regarding the DSM, parents, families, and caregivers can enter healthcare settings armed with knowledge about the DSM, how it is used, and what its ideologies are founded upon. Having an idea of the pros and cons of the manual will help you determine whether you want to embrace all information rendered to you through the DSM. You will be able to make better informed decisions because you now understand the criticisms of a manual that has often been promoted as the "bible," the answer to all mental illness and behavior.

Chapter 4

Criminalizing the mentally ill: Why a serious discussion of assisted psychiatric care is overdue

ylan Andrew Quick, age 20, began stabbing fourteen of his fellow classmates with a utility knife in April of 2013 at Lone Star College in Cypress, Texas. After confessing that he had been fantasying about "stabbing people to death" since the age of 8, it became apparent that he has a history of untreated mental illness. Not only was Quick nonchalant about the attack, but he also stated that he had been planning this for quite "some time." Quick was taken to a psychiatric hospital and received a psychological evaluation to determine the state of his mental health and to garner a mental health history. He was charged with three counts of aggravated assault with a deadly weapon. Quick will more than likely not receive much needed psychiatric treatment, but will end up in jail, criminalized.

In April of 2013, Eugene Maraventano (age 64) brutally murdered his wife, Janet Maraventano, and 27-year-old son, Bryan Maraventano, with a knife due to paranoid beliefs that he contracted HIV from unscrupulous relationships with prostitutes. Mr. Maraventano also attempted suicide but according to reports, failed on each attempt. He called 911 four days following the murders. Reports show that he stated to a 911 dispatcher that "I killed my wife and I killed my son; I can't kill myself." Multiple reports also show that court documents do not provide proof that Maraventano had HIV.

May 26, 2007, Jeanette Tiggs received a call that would forever change her life. Jason West, a Cleveland Heights Ohio Police Officer, responded to a call regarding a street fight. Upon arrival to the scene and witnessing an unknown vehicle pulling into a nearby driveway on May 25, West blocked the vehicle with his cruiser and stepped out only to be greeted with the gun of 27-year-old Timothy Halton, Jr., the son of Jeanette Tiggs. Although Halton received a sentence of four years' probation for murdering a Police Officer, it is important to note that he has suffered from schizophrenia and has a long history of violent, unruly behavior. Prior to the murder, Ms. Tiggs witnessed withdrawal and violent temperament as a result of not taking his medication. She knew his behavior would finally lead to something she had dreaded many days of her life. On May 26, 2007 her worst nightmare because her reality.

One of my own cases as a therapist had a rather heartbreaking ending as well. At the time, I worked with high school age kids when I encountered one of the most difficult cases I had ever worked with. I had a 18-year-old girl, Kayce, who was diagnosed with oppositional defiant disorder, ADHD, and bipolar disorder. Her mother called me one morning after waking up to her most dreaded nightmare, her only daughter standing over her with an iron bat while she slept. Her daughter intended to harm, maybe even murder, she and her 1-year-old son. Although Kayce was getting along with peers in group therapy, she was totally different in other settings. Not only would she beat her mother and threaten to kill her brother almost daily, she exhibited extreme outbursts in school and at home. On a few occasions, I feared for my own safety. In the end, this mother was faced with two decisions: turn her daughter in to the police (making her a criminal) or commit her to a residential treatment facility (making her a patient).

These stories would certainly provoke anti-stigma extremists to question my validity, goal, and stance on mental illness. They would also provoke them to point out that a direct relationship between violence and mental illness has not been proven. To have such narrow views would be to undermine the reality that while violence does not characterize all cases involving severe or untreated mental illness, these cases provide proof of our need to implement better treatment options for those cases that do. We cannot ignore individuals who may be too impaired to make rational decisions, protect themselves, and reframe from harming others. While we love to embrace "higher functioning" individuals in our minds, we cannot exclude the "lower functioning." The above and similar cases show much more than mere lack of judgment or coincidences. You can frequent almost every news channel throughout the day and run into a story of this magnitude or greater. You can also visit your local NAMI or support group and hear a family discuss their lack of ability to influence the system. These stories are not rare occurrences. Although the media has a reputation of sensationalizing stories of defeat and violence, the reality is that untreated and severe mental illness exists and is more real than we care to admit. The above cases are becoming an aspect of our daily lives. Many parents, families, and caregivers are experiencing the helplessness, fear, and uncertainty of Jeanette Tiggs. They dread a phone call, a report about their worst nightmare.

There are too many cases involving severe need and few answers for those who are homelessness, victimized, violent, or incarcerated. What is pivotal in cases such as the above is not only self-knowledge but support and love from family, friends, and healthcare providers. However, in many cases, such support is often missing and parents, families, and caregivers must ride out the storm alone. There are a few things I would encourage all families in this position to do:

- Have a candid discussion with your loved one: You don't want these discussions, which should be loving, open, and honest, to turn into arguments or confrontations. But you do want to gather those who are concerned and have a discussion. If your loved one doesn't think they have a problem, try to examine where this is coming from (denial, fear, lack of knowledge, rebelliousness, anger, or lack of insight). If any of these things are blocking your loved one's perception of their illness, arming yourself with knowledge on how to help is even more important.

- Learn how to identify warning signs: One thing Jeanette Tiggs did was recognize the behavioral changes in her son (violent temperament and withdrawal), which signaled he was getting sick again. You want to learn how to recognize the warning signs of your loved one and depending on the severity of your loved one's illness, teach them to recognize signs as well. The faster you can identify impairment, the faster you can attempt to stop and treat it.

o Have an outlet: One of the most important things you need as the "head coach" of your family is time to refuel yourself, your mind, and your soul. Take seriously your need for counseling (spiritual/Christian or general), support through support groups, time alone, time to journal or engage in light-hearted activities, family time, and self-care. One thing a combat warrior does during battle to recharge himself is lay low.

o Accept that you can encounter a crisis or emergency any day, any time: Walking through life not believing a tragedy can occur in your own life is like driving without looking in your side mirrors. You don't want to walk in fear, but you do want to walk in reality.

o Have a plan: Write down, in a notebook, things you could do if an emergency occurs. For example, if your loved one begins to hallucinate, write down what your first step will be. Will it be discussion with your loved one? Will it be hospitalization? Will it be calling a doctor? Have your loved one contribute, if possible.

o Know what you will do and say: When emergencies occur, it's really easy to say and do whatever comes to mind, I'm guilty of this myself! But you want to have some idea of what you will do such as speaking calming words to someone out of control, reminding yourself of something that can keep you calm, or acting calm even when you aren't.

o Know who you will contact: It's always best to have emergency numbers of local healthcare centers, or hospital ER's. close by. Have a list of family members or friends you will contact and put it in a safe place. For kids, you can develop a "tool kit" of emergency contacts using paper, post-it notes, and a box.

o Know how you will subdue threatening behavior: In cases of severe mental illness where violence is a possibility, be vigilant and know what you will do. It's difficult for people to associate violence with those they love, but an illness can cause the person to behave differently from their typical way of relating to others, increasing the possibility of violence. Not being able to tolerate frustration increases escalation of anger and maybe violence.

While these things are extremely important, involuntary outpatient or court-ordered treatment includes laws that will make a world of difference in the lives of suffering individuals who are harmful to themselves and others. Unfortunately, there is widespread lack of knowledge about court-ordered treatment and because of this there is strong resistance. Let's learn more about court-ordered treatment, two states that have implemented it successfully, and why stricter options are necessary.

Why we need better treatment options

Involuntary treatment (or 302) involves the commitment of an individual with a psychiatric condition who is determined by hospital criteria to be a danger to self or others or otherwise unable to care for basic needs (food, clothing, shelter, etc.). When a 302 occurs, an individual is committed to a psychiatric hospital against their will for only 72hrs. During this time, healthcare providers stabilize the individual and provide needed treatment. Involuntary commitment, as discussed in chapter 2, is extremely difficult for families. As a result, a form of court-ordered treatment, which allows individuals to remain in the community while being treated, has been proposed by various leading professionals in the mental health industry. Assisted Outpatient Treatment (AOT) (also known as mandated outpatient treatment, court ordered treatment, involuntary outpatient commitment, or community treatment orders) is a form of treatment utilized for high-risk, high-needs populations to increase treatment adherence (e.g., medication usage or therapy attendance). Individuals are ordered by a judge to follow a treatment order (outpatient therapy sessions) and if the order is not followed the court can petition an individual to receive a psychiatric evaluation

to determine "imminent risk" to society or self. The purpose
of AOT is to divert individuals from inpatient care or the
criminal justice system. Several states have already enacted
AOT laws including several countries such as Canada, Israel,
United Kingdom, Australia, and New Zealand (Swartz &
Swanson, 2004). Research suggests that AOT is a viable
solution to severe mental illness and may be our only hope
for helping high risk populations. AOT is recognized as an
intervention to prevent readmission to hospitals and reduce
incidents of homelessness, unnecessary criminalization,
violence due to perceptual difficulties, and victimization.

Why court-ordered treatment?

In the winter of 1999, a man with a history of repeated
hospitalizations and mental illness (by the name of Andrew
Goldstein) pushed Kendra Webdale onto Manhattan's
subway tracks in New York city. Kendra never saw it coming.
Not only were Kendra's parents devastated but Governor
George Pataki immediately pushed to enact a law that would
require individuals with severe and untreated mental illness, a
history of hospitalizations, or violence to receive treatment in
the community. According to the Office of Mental Health
(n.d.) 2,433 court-orders have been issued for AOT. The
process to begin a court-order involves someone filing a
petition designed to identify those who are in need and
unable to care for themselves without supervision. The
petition is jumpstarted by a doctor who completes what is
known as a treatment plan (a plan designed by therapists,
doctors, or psychiatrists to explain the needs of the patient
and to offer objectives as well as goals to be reached before
treatment is aborted). The process also involves a hearing

where all evidence is evaluated, testimony is offered by a doctor, and, if possible, the person alleged to need treatment (before a final decision is made) is present. If it is found that the individual for which the hearing is being held needs treatment, an order will be issued to a doctor, Director of a mental health facility, or hospital where treatment will be monitored and received. The order is valid up to six months. The process of filing a petition and pursuing court-ordered treatment varies according to state. It should also be made clear that these provisions do not force medication.

A prescribed plan for treatment is important for individuals with an unstable severe or untreated mental illness. AOT has been repeatedly promoted by the Treatment Advocacy Center (TAC), Mental Illness Policy Org, New York, and parts of California. These supporters believe that AOT would properly assist individuals not aware of the severity and instability of their mental impairment. When individuals have trouble functioning due to an un-stabilized mental illness, many families are met with resistance, resentment, and rage when they attempt to seek outside help. In extreme cases, a family cannot coerce their loved one into treatment or to take much needed medication without an argument, which often leaves the family in danger or without hope. As a result, we need more progressive mental health treatment options for sufferers. AOT reduces the possibility of a negative outcome. About 44 states in the U.S. have AOT laws authorizing courts to order individuals with severe, untreated mental illness into treatment. Six states do not have AOT laws. These states include: Connecticut, Nevada, Maryland, New Mexico, Tennessee, and Massachusetts, according to the Treatment Advocacy Center. Proponents of AOT claim that the intervention has the ability to improve treatment compliance and reduce readmissions to hospitals involuntarily. Munetz and colleagues evaluated the social functioning of a group of 24 individuals who had a high rate of recidivism and found positive results when AOT was implemented (as cited in Swartz & Swanson, 2004, p.587). According to Swartz and Swanson (2004) "in a 12-month follow-up period, outpatient committed patients demonstrated reduced emergency room visits, reduced hospital readmission, and reduced lengths of stay" (p.587). Others claim that court-ordered treatment can be useful in the community because it is an "intermediate step between hospitalization and total autonomy that mandates some level of supervision, and includes steps such as therapy, participation in treatment programs, supervised living arrangements, or the acceptance of psychiatric medication" (Strang, 2009, p.248). Court-orders are severely needed in our communities today. With repeated homicide and suicide media reports almost every day and the perpetual issue of treatment noncompliance, the implementation of assisted outpatient treatment is way overdue. As a result, New York City's Kendra's Law and California's Laura's Law have been implemented in addition to similar laws in other states.

Criteria for Kendra's Law

Many critics of AOT continue to promote the view that it imprisons individuals and forces treatment on those who are capable of making decisions on their own. Sadly, this view has created resistance to much needed change and remains very narrow. AOT is for the most vulnerable among us. What critics fail to consider is that individuals who are homeless, incarcerated, or victimized are not capable of appreciating their liberties due to the consequences of a severe mental impairment. These highly vulnerable individuals are unable to care for themselves. AOT provides impaired individuals with greater liberty because treatment prevents negative consequences that could rob an individual of their ultimate freedom. If an individual ends up incarcerated, homeless, or dead, how then can these individuals appreciate their "civil liberties?"

The majority of resistance stems from individuals who are afraid of losing independence and ultimately control. But if these individuals had a greater understanding of how AOT laws are implemented in other states, they may find themselves succumbing to the helpfulness of the law. Let's take a look at New York City's Kendra's Law and California's Laura's Law. According to the New York Office Of Mental Health, Kendra's Law requires that individuals meet the following criteria with convincing evidence before AOT orders are placed:

- o Is at least 18 years old
- o Is suffering from a mental illness
- o Is unlikely to survive safely in the community without supervision, based on a clinical determination
- o Has a history of lack of compliance with mental health treatment for a mental illness that has: (prior to the filing of the petition and at least twice within the last 36-months) been a significant factor in necessitating psychiatric hospitalization, or receipt of services in a forensic or other mental health unit of a correctional facility or a local correctional facility. Or prior to the filing of the petition, resulted in one of more acts of serious violent behavior toward self or others or threats of, or attempts at, serious physical harm to self or

others within the last 48-months, and is, as a result of his or her mental illness, unlikely to voluntarily participate in the outpatient treatment that would enable him or her to live safely in the community. In view of his or her treatment history and current behavior, is in need of assisted outpatient treatment in order to prevent a relapse or deterioration which would be likely to result in serious harm to a person or others and is likely to benefit from assisted outpatient treatment.

A court may not issue an AOT order unless it finds that AOT is the least restrictive alternative available for an individual. Other aspects of Kendra's law include a written treatment plan by a physician (i.e., a plan on how treatment is to be pursued), a court hearing to look at all the evidence, and a disposition hearing needed to determine if AOT is ultimately needed and if all evidence provides support for the requested court order for treatment.

Criteria for Laura's Law

California allows for court ordered treatment in certain counties such as Nevada County where Laura Wilcox was murdered. A revision of the law was considered by state legislature during the spring of 2013 to implement changes to protect individuals unable to protect themselves. The legislative change, for example, would remove the requirement that only the county board of supervisors authorize the need for treatment, but also allow the county's Department of Public Health to implement the law.

Adjustments would ensure that Laura's law is being utilized effectively. In order for someone to be court-ordered into treatment using Laura's law, the following must occur:

o   For inpatient care, there must be a danger to self/others or inability to provide for basic personal needs for food, clothing, or shelter.

o   For outpatient care in counties that have adopted Laura's Law, the individual must have a condition likely to:

> o substantially deteriorate
> o be unlikely to survive safely in the community without supervision
> o have a history of noncompliance that includes two hospitalizations in the past 36 months
> o act/threaten/attempt violence to self/others in 48 months immediately preceding a petition filing
> o be likely to need treatment to prevent meeting inpatient standard(s)
> o be likely to benefit from assisted treatment.

o   For care in counties that have not implemented Laura's Law, there currently are no legal mechanisms for AOT.

With greater knowledge about the law, what it offers, how it is utilized, and what benefits and even negative consequences can result, will help you understand why families should support similar laws in their state or region. To learn more details about Laura's Law go to: http://www.lauraslawoc.org.

Reasons why states should mimic Kendra's and Laura's law

Noncompliance, medication adherence, and similar difficulties

Most families caring for a loved one with a severe or untreated mental illness are comforted by AOT in their state. However, anxiety arises when families question how long the AOT orders will last. There is often a failure of individuals with severe or untreated mental health problems to comply with aftercare, medication, and other necessary services. Another anxiety-provoking dilemma is when a sufferer rejects or resists the court-order. The great part about AOT is that it provides little to no room for individuals to resist the order if it is determined, by the courts, that the order is severely needed. Noncompliance with psychiatric treatment has become a major issue in regards to medication adherence, outpatient therapy attendance, and case management services. Most individuals who have received either residential or group home treatment or some kind of inpatient treatment return to families and caregivers who are largely unprepared, unsuspecting, and uninformed. As a result, families end up tackling the mental health system alone, trying to help their loved one keep appointments or prevent their loved one from returning to inpatient care. In most cases, families have little say in the treatment of their loved one and often end up begging the system to let them help their loved one. Because of state statutes, families are no longer "valued members" of care. As a result, individuals who were never really capable of caring for themselves are given responsibility to care for themselves. Unfortunately, such individuals begin to exhibit noncompliance with medication, therapy attendance, or case management meetings. AOT laws that are properly enforced will help families secure treatment or help individuals of legal age make decisions that are ultimately in their best interest. Without AOT, individuals who are incapable of caring for themselves will often find themselves homeless, criminalized, victimized, homicidal, or self-injurious. Bentley, Rosenson, and Zito (1990) state that "because adherence to medication often plays a crucial role in reducing symptoms, preventing or forestalling rehospitalization, and increasing prosocial behavior in patients, strategies must be developed to promote compliance" (p.274). While strategies such as psycho-education (educating patients and families to the importance of complying with treatment) and bibliography (reading materials on treatment) are important, one very significant strategy has been the implementation of involuntary outpatient treatment or AOT. Even if individuals are educated to the importance of treatment compliance, they still have the "freedom" to reject treatment. Therefore, psychoeducation alone is not a reliable remedy for the severely disabled, we need changed laws and people to enforce them. AOT treats the most severe and removes the ability for severely impaired individuals to reject treatment. It is better to have a loved one within a system that court-orders treatment, than a system that criminalizes its mentally ill inmates.

Parents, families, and caregivers also face difficulty in getting their loved ones to take their prescribed medication.

There are multiple reasons for this such as dislike of side effects, lack of understanding of the importance of taking meds on a schedule, desire for independence or "normalcy," lack of supervision, and forgetfulness. Noncompliance with medication has become a major issue in medicine (Bulloch, Adair, & Patten, p.720). This is one of the reasons why I encourage parents, families, and caregivers to research the medications of their loved ones and understand the purpose for the medication. You can go to the Online Drug Index at www.rxlist.com or www.drugs.com for further information about medication. This site is very easy to navigate. Go to the search engine, type in the name of the medication, and multiple search results will appear. If you go to drugs.com, you can also just click on "Drugs A-Z" to look at a list of medications.

Researchers Bulloch, Adair, and Patten (2006) state that "noncompliance manifests itself in several ways, including failure to fill a prescription, failure to take any medication, early discontinuation of medication (dropout), and failure to regularly take prescribed dosages" (p.220). Not only is it difficult for healthcare providers, parents, families, and caregivers to encourage medication adherence, but it is also very difficult to motivate individuals who have been in inpatient settings to comply with aftercare (e.g., outpatient treatment, community mental health treatment, or case management services). As discussed in chapter 2, individuals who are receiving inpatient care are supervised and treated. Once an individual leaves this structured, supervised environment they begin to refuse further treatment, stop taking medications, and stop attending therapy. While most noncompliance is due to the individual's illness and lack of insight, it could also be due to lack of fit between the individual and treatment setting. For example, an individual who is suffering from a substance abuse disorder and contacts a random clinic for treatment may be assessed and treated for depression or bipolar disorder, not their substance abuse. If the counselor or agency does not offer services for substance abuse, the individual may drop out of treatment feeling that their most pressing need isn't being met.

Treatment compliance is important, which is why AOT has been proposed by leading specialists in the field of mental health. The outcome for individuals who reject treatment is grim. Owen, Rutherford, Jones, Tennant, and Smallman (1997) state that "court-ordered treatment after criminal offenses confirmed that the treatment refusers in that population had a worse outcome in terms of higher re-hospitalization rate, higher re-arrest rates or homelessness at 5 year follow up" (p.26). AOT offers a layer of protection for individuals suffering from severe or untreated mental health and families who struggle to secure treatment for their loved one. AOT provides families with options, options they never had before.

In the next section, we will briefly discuss what research has shown is the consequences of untreated mental health. We will also briefly discuss how we can help implement change.

The result of minimal options for psychiatric treatment

Criminalization

During the early colonial times (pre-1776) individuals with severe and untreated mental health disorders were left to care for themselves or left to be cared for by jailhouses and other facilities used to hold "criminals." Our current juvenile and criminal justice system is criminalizing the mentally ill and diverting them from much needed treatment. The United States Department of Justice reports that a study done by the Council of State Governments Justice Center (2009) showed that 16.9% of adults in a sample of local jails were found to have a serious mental illness, about 3-6 times the rate of the general population. Sadly, many individuals who commit crimes and have a history of mental health problems, rarely if ever receive treatment while incarcerated. Many of our jails and prisons overflow with untreated mentally ill inmates, while hospitals close and continue to support movements to

Image 3: Ref. ID 10036755: Individual behind iron cell

sustain short-term treatment. Mental health remains a challenge for the juvenile and criminal justice system. Another major problem is a lack of knowledge among our police force. They need training to protect themselves and others. Knowledge equals less brutality. It is also difficult to prevent inmates with a long history of mental illness from returning to jail. If a mental illness is not treated, the root of the problem is never dealt with. Once an inmate is released from prison untreated, they will more than likely reengage in antisocial and problematic behaviors that will lead to incarceration once again. This is the revolving door of the juvenile and criminal justice system. With better treatment options and promotion of greater education on mental illness, we as a society can help reduce the criminalization of the mentally ill.

Victimization

Individuals with severe mental illness are considered a vulnerable population. Like other vulnerable populations (children, homeless, and elderly), individuals with severe or untreated mental illness are highly susceptible to dangers all around them such as crime and incarceration. Most studies on victimization and mental illness focus on domestic violence, but victimization occurs in many areas. Poor judgment, impulsivity which can lead to confrontation, and living conditions or place of residence can all lead to victimization. Some individuals with severe or untreated mental illness are homeless, living in dilapidated conditions, or choosing strangers to live with. In severe cases, individuals can also be victimized by law enforcement who lack the appropriate training to deal properly with a resistant, noncompliant individual. Teplin, McClelland, Abram, and Weiner (2005) states that individuals with severe mental illness are vulnerable because of "…impaired reality testing, disorganized thought processes, impulsivity, and poor planning, and problem solving, [which] can compromise one's ability to perceive risks and protect oneself" (p2). Research also suggests a correlation between victimization and substance abuse, conflicted social relationships, poverty, and homelessness (Teplin, McClelland, Abram, & Weiner, 2005).

Homelessness

Many people believe that homelessness occurs as a result of a lack of motivation, substance abuse, or socioeconomic status and poverty. However, the reality is often that homelessness could be the result of childhood or adult abuse, past or present trauma, and severe, persistent, or untreated mental illness among many other factors. The National Center On Family Homelessness reports that 1 in 45 kids (1.6 million) are homeless in America. According to the National Alliance To End Homelessness (2013), about 250,000 families are homeless, while a significant portion of the homeless are young parents. Our homeless population not only has to combat mental illness and worry about securing things for

Image 4: Ref. ID1002211: The Great Depression   95 | P a g e

their basic needs (food, clothing, shelter, safety), but also the stigmatized perceptions of an uneducated and unmerciful society.

Negative perceptions about the homeless population and their ability to be productive citizens of society further marginalize the individual who is already stigmatized by their mental illness. In fact, Wild (2006) uses the term "market failure" to describe the "tendency for already vulnerable people to become further marginalized by negative economic events such as rising rents or job loss" (p.78). For individuals experiencing severe or untreated mental illness including comorbid issues such as substance abuse, it can be difficult for them to secure and maintain employment, pay bills on time, and keep up with their basic needs. When an individual has a severe illness that impairs perception and decision making ability such as bipolar disorder, it can be extremely difficult to keep these individuals off the street. In some cases, extravagant spending sprees, failing to pay rent and other bills, risky and impulsive behavior, gambling behaviors, substance abuse, violence, sexual indiscretion, and confrontational behaviors all place this individual at risk for making bad choices and ending up on the streets. Some literature points to trans-institutionalization, the process by which an individual ends up in various institutions (psychiatric, rehabilitation, or prison) as opposed to ending up in their own communities or homes, as the major problem of homelessness. I believe that the revolving door of the mental health and prison systems are by far the biggest problem with trans-institutionalization. Many individuals with a severe or untreated psychiatric illness often end up cycling between the psychiatric and prison system for the majority of their lives. In cases such as these, better discharge planning involving housing or court-ordered treatment would allow families to petition the courts to provide treatment and encourage a suffering individual to get help, whether in the community or another suitable psychiatric setting. The unpredictability of severe mental illness requires continuity of care.

Violence

In 2005, 5,668 youths between the ages of ten and fourteen were murdered, an average of sixteen deaths each day (CDC, 2008). Homicide was the second leading cause of death for individuals between the ages of ten and fourteen (Youth Violence, 2008). Even more devastating is that "persons under the age of 25 accounted for 52.0% of those arrested for murder and 64.8% of those arrested for robbery in 2006" (as cited in Youth Violence, 2008). Troubled children and adolescents find themselves entangled within the juvenile justice system in need of a range of mental health assessments. The National Institute of Mental Health (2009) estimated that 1 in 10 children suffer from a severe mental disorder, severe enough to cause impairment. This impairment creates poor judgment which can then lead to violence and bad decisions. According to the Surgeon General's Report on violence and mental health (2009), a study done in Denver showed a relationship between violent behavior among youths and mental health problems based on the responses of parents from the Child Behavior Checklist. Multiple problems were reported in this study such as externalizing behaviors (violence, fighting, confrontations), obsessive compulsive behavior, lack of communication, aggressiveness, social withdrawal, depression, and hyperactivity. Rates of these psychological problems in non-delinquent youths were lower according to this study.

Conclusion

Incarceration, victimization, violence, and homelessness are four important consequences of poor mental health treatment. Multiple studies have pointed to this correlation. Further research is needed to prove causation. Until then, smart thinkers realize that we need to alter our current treatment options available to needy families. AOT attempts to offer hope and gives individuals with severe or untreated mental illness a second chance. If policy makers, educators, advocates, and others in power become more informed about AOT and appropriately monitor its benefits or lack of benefits, we can offer many families a stable recourse. In order to reduce the unfair criminalization of those in need of psychiatric attention, we must first promote the use of treatment options that help divert suffers into the mental health system and not the prison system. In failing to promote and support treatment options for severe or untreated mental health, we indirectly send the message that we do not believe stronger treatment options are needed and that we don't care about the future of America's severely impaired. I believe there are three significant ways to positively impact our current and failed mental health system. We can certainly advocate, in our state, for attention to these suggested remedies:

1. Reform civil commitment laws and enforce/redefine Assisted Outpatient Treatment (AOT):

- o Enhanced civil commitment laws would increase timely treatment by overturning the "dangerousness" criteria.

- AOT in every state would offer the option of court-ordered outpatient and also inpatient treatment including medication management.

- Enhanced laws would ensure that individuals would not end up homeless, incarcerated, or victimized, but receive proper treatment.

2. *Increase age of consent for treatment:*

- Youths (ages 14 or 16) are granted legal authority by the state to make treatment decisions or refuse treatment. Many youths lack the maturity to make appropriate decisions on their healthcare.

- The responsibility to pursue, refuse, or modify psychiatric treatment should remain in the sole control of the adult parent or caregiver until an individual is 18 years of age.

3. *Provide education and resources for families and caregivers:*

- At an initial mental health assessment, all individuals should be given information about free mental health services in the community. Unfortunately, when families are assessed, they are often sent away with an appointment card, referral services, pamphlets, and other promotional brochures about the agency. Most agencies will not provide families with external resources to find further information such as websites, magazines, or newsletters.

AOT makes is possible for individuals to receive psychiatric care if they are actively psychotic or impaired and unable to care for their basic needs. No individual would be committed, under the current proposed AOT laws, against their will unless there was reasonable amount of suspicion to assume that an individual is actively psychotic and unable to remain safely in the community. The ultimate goal of court-ordered treatment is to enhance treatment compliance, reduce homelessness, incarceration or reduce recidivism among those previously incarcerated, decrease victimization and violence, and offer more options to families who are concerned about their loved one. A discussion of better treatment options is way overdue. It is a discussion we need to finally intervene and also change the outcome of the lives of those who have no idea of their impending doom. It is up to those of us who are in good health to reach out and touch the lives of those who are not in good health. You may not be able to make immediate change, but you can certainly make your mark by advocating in your state and becoming knowledgeable about discrepancies in our system so that you can share them with others. Resisting the political pressure of people who have different views from you, is also something I encourage you to do. A political battle is intense, ugly, and unfair. Stand on the truth that you have. I call you to action today.

Chapter 5

Bullying prevention: Legally protecting children with special needs

Bullying has become an epidemic among children and adolescents. About 3.2 million kids are victims of bullying every year and 160,000 adolescents skip school every day to avoid being bullied. Bullying can encompass a wide variety of behaviors and often fall in to four major categories:

- o Cyber (the use of social media such as Twitter, MySpace, Facebook)
- o Verbal (name calling)
- o Social (ostracizing, making others feel left out, spreading rumors)
- o Physical (hitting, kicking, punching, etc.)

Many parents only pay attention to the most noticeable forms of bullying such as name calling or physical aggression. But it is important that parents and families also pay great attention to social and cyber bullying. Reports show that cyber bullying has become as much of a problem as more common types of bullying. Cyber bullying is a rather insidious type of assault because it is often hidden from adults. Amanda Todd, a Canadian teenager, reportedly committed suicide as a result of repeated cyber bullying. She designed a comprehensive YouTube video prior to her death in order to express the emotional pain and psychological imprisonment she experienced at the hands of her peers. You can find her video at: http://bit.ly/RiQ1Th.

Bullying is defined as "unwanted and aggressive behavior among school aged children that involves a real or perceived threat." It leads to poor mental and emotional health, self-esteem, post-traumatic stress disorder, difficulty learning, high levels of anxiety, depression, and even high blood pressure. There are psychological, emotional, and physiological consequences of being the victim of frequent bullying. It is often difficult to connect attempted and completed suicides to bullying. But studies show that suicide is often found among children and adolescents who experience depression, anxiety, and other types of mental and behavioral disorders. Suicide is the 3rd leading cause of death for individuals between the age of 15 and 24 years old. Kids who are anxious or depressed are also sometimes bullied. Anxiety and depression can lead to suicidal thoughts. One way to prevent the negative consequences of bullying is to understand what contributes to the behavior of aggressive youth.

What contributes to bullying?

Having worked within school-based programs, my experience has been that there are three important components that contribute to the behavioral development of youths who bully:

- o Environment: For children and adolescents who come from negative environments or experience a lack of positive role models, poor adult supervision, negative peer influence, drug activity, and anti-social behaviors, it is difficult to position themselves in the world positively. Having experienced short-term bullying myself, I understand the profound impact of environment on behavior. As an 8-year-old I would visit my great grandmother who was suffering from severe Alzheimer's Disease at the time. My mother had to be her caretaker while my grandmother worked. During that time, I would play with some of the children in her neighborhood. Being a home-schooled child living in a middle class neighborhood, I became an immediate threat. While most of the kids liked my younger sibling and I, I was frequently harassed by one child by phone, physically assaulted by two boys in the neighborhood, and slapped by a female 3 years my senior. After my mother requested to speak with multiple parents, I realized while visiting their homes that these individuals were not necessarily cold-hearted kids. In fact, they had difficult lives that contributed to a negative worldview, low self-esteem, oppositional behavior, and anger. Many disliked their lives and wanted what they perceived I had.

o Mental and behavioral health: Most of society fails to recognize the importance of considering the mental and behavioral health of frequent bullies. Not all kids bully because they are impacted by a negative environment. Some kids bully because they are not properly treated for a problem that controls most of their behavior toward others. Research shows that children who have been diagnosed with ADHD are more likely to bully than kids who are not. Other disorders such as oppositional defiant disorder or conduct disorder can motivate assaultive behavior as well.

o Self-efficacy/self-esteem: Some youths, who cannot recognize their full potential, are hurting so much that they lash out at other kids when the opportunity presents itself. These kids require adult supervision and intervention. They also can benefit from a caring adult who is dedicated to helping them see their potential. The saying "misery loves company" applies here. In other cases, kids who believe and have been told they are better engage in bullying others they perceive are inferior to themselves. In either case, self-esteem is the trigger for this assaultive behavior.

Tools for confronting assaultive behaviors in the educational system

Because bullying is becoming an epidemic in multiple areas of the world, primarily the United States, it is important that society consider various options for protecting children with special needs, children unable to care for themselves. With the implementation of the Individualized Education Plan (IEP), it is easier for parents to request special accommodations for their children and request someone monitor their child during the day due to frequent encounters with bullying. However, there are many parents who feel unheard in the educational system when the topic of bullying prevention is raised. As a result, many parents are investigating ways to protect their children. There are laws and special considerations within the educational system for children with special needs, but most parents are uninformed about their rights or the rights of their child. There are six things parents can do to help protect their children from bullying situations:

o   Know your federal rights: Children with special needs have federal rights laws to protect them. When children are badgered by peers, staff, school teachers, or other individuals because of a disability, parents have the right to pursue in a court of law what is known as "disability harassment." Complaints are filed through the Office for Civil Rights (OCR) this is a civil rights case. The OCR supports both 504 of the Rehabilitation Act of 1973 (referred to as 'Section 504') and Title II of the Americans with Disabilities Act of 1990 (Title II), which were enacted to protect children with special needs from being treated impartially in the educational system. Children with an IEP or 504 plan would be protected under these federal laws. Parents can file a complained with the OCR by visiting:

- http://www2.ed.gov/about/offices/list/ocr /complaintintro.html
- http://www.hhs.gov/ocr/civilrights/compl aints/index.html.

You can mail or fax a complaint to your regional office to the attention of "OCR Regional Manager. You can visit the OCR online for specific location details at http://www.hhs.gov/ocr/office/about/rgn-hqaddresses.html or dial (800) 368-1019. If you have questions, concerns, or need clarification, you can email the OCR at OCRMail@hhs.gov. Keep in mind that some complaints must be filed within 180 days of when the violation occurred.

To learn more about disability rights, visit https://www.disability.gov/civil_rights. An important job of the OCR is to prevent discrimination and mistreatment of individuals with special needs and other mental health problems.

The OCR is a resource that you want to keep near. You also want to learn how to contact your state OCR. I encourage you to learn more about the OCR, the Americans With Disabilities Act, 504 plans, and IEP's and share with other families, parents, and caregivers. Sometimes these individuals learn best when information is coming from people in their shoes.

- o Write the Principal or School District: This is something both you and your child can do. There is

WHAT EVERY PARENT, FAMILY, & CAREGIVER
SHOULD KNOW

definitely some psychology to your child writing his or her Principal about being bullied. A child can have a major impact on most adults and when they express what bothers them, adults respond. Encourage your child to write a genuine letter about being bullied and follow-up with a letter of your own. Not only are you encouraging your child to be proactive, but you are also expressing to the school that you are an engaged parent who wants to see change. Don't forget to contact your school each time your child is bullied. Doing this helps create a track record.

o   Develop a list of trusted adults: Consider sitting down with your child and developing a list of people in the school, community, or neighborhood who can act as a resource or supporter at times when your child needs adult intervention. Allowing a child to list the names of people they trust and feel comfortable with, will encourage them to seek help when necessary.

o   Teach kids about proper boundaries: This may seem to be a common sense action that doesn't need explaining. But some parents forget to teach their children the importance of identifying inappropriate relationships. Because children want to have friends, feel accepted, and fit in, they will most likely compromise and be a victim in a bad relationship. Kids need to be reminded of the importance of positive relationships that are stable and healthy.

o   Role play: While working with children in a middle school environment, I constructed game cards using

107 | P a g e

index cards with bullying scenarios. The kids also helped me construct scenarios. The kids were each given parts to role play as both the victim and the bully. After the game we discussed the scenarios and I was amazed to see just how much they had learned. The purpose of role play is to put the individual in the situation before they actually have to be in the situation. You are providing practice so that if the child has to encounter a bully, they can think back to your role playing and consider more appropriate ways to handle the situation. You can also create scenarios that entail both positive and negative responses to a bully. This can help kids see just how their responses can positively or negatively impact the outcome. The purpose of this activity is to provide "practice" and build confidence.

o   Meet with the Principal: Contact your school's Principal for a meeting and allow your child to go with you. Opening lines of communication and pulling down barriers may require a meeting with the head of the school. This meeting may entail you introducing yourself and your child, asking questions about the school's policy on bullying, or meeting with teachers and other personnel. If you develop a cordial rapport with the school Principal, it may be easier to discuss more sensitive issues such as bullying.

o   Change schools or home-school: In some cases, an alternative education or a change in environment is the only remedy. Kids are in school to learn, not fight. Bullying distracts kids from growing appropriately and reduces self-esteem. Do what you must.

There are also more strict actions that schools can take to protect children from harassment. My prevention efforts are focused on encouraging schools to consider the following:

- o Develop mandatory six week classes: It has always been quite interesting to me that school systems have sex education, educational on evolution, and other classes deemed "important." If these classes are taught to kids as highly relevant, then classes on the psychological effects of bullying and the importance of prevention are also significant. Classes should be mandatory in certain school districts where bullying rates are high. Classes should be offered to children, adolescents, and families during convenient times. This is a proactive step toward eradicating aggressive behavior and educating families about the seriousness of bullying. The National Bullying Prevention Center reports that studies show 50% of bullying incidents stop when another peer steps in. It is important to teach kids how powerful their intervening on the behalf of another peer can be.

- o Court-order frequent bullies into treatment: Youths who are being reared in negative environments and whose parents cannot or will not correct aggressive behavior, should be court-ordered by the school district into behavior modification classes. If a child or adolescent continues to bully despite legal, school, and community consequences, psychotherapy and behavior management classes should be offered to families.

o Implement strict consequences for parents/guardians: Some parents will not or cannot control the aggressive behavior of their children. Despite attempts to reduce aggression, some parents give up. In cases such as this, it is important for the school district to step in with court-ordered behavior management or psychotherapy. These parents are obviously in need of external help. It is important to develop parental consequences that will coerce families into taking more responsibility. According to the National Bullying Prevention Center, the effects of bullying can result in high drop-out rates, lack of interest in academics, inability to concentrate, decrease in grades, and high rates of absenteeism. As a result, there should be consequences for parents of aggressive children. When some kids feel pressure, they turn to lethal means.

Suicide is becoming the method of choice for many adolescents who are tired of being bullied. Rehtaeh Parsons, a Canadian girl, engaged in a suicide attempt that resulted in her death after frequent bullying and what her parents alleged to be a rape by four boys. Her parents stated that Rehtaeh was deeply depressed by the rape and felt rejected by her community. The mother has reported to various media outlets that one of the perpetrators of the rape took a picture of the incident and distributed it to the school and community. The family reported that the bullying escalated so much that relocation was their only means of escape. The prosecutors in the case decided not to make this a criminal case and pursue charges. Consider the case from chapter 4 about Dylan Quick, the young man charged with stabbing 14 of his fellow classmates in April of 2013. Multiple reports claim that Quick had been bullied as a result of a hearing impairment.

Conclusion

It is important to understand your rights. You can find thousands of reputable resources online. You can also find further resources at the sites listed in this chapter by looking for a "resources" page. Many sites link to other sites. I also encourage you to keep a record of cases involving bullying where victims have committed suicide, sustained multiple injuries, or retaliated in negative ways. This information can be useful for school districts considering changes to their policies. This information can also be useful for others advocating for anti-bullying laws. One way to keep a record may be to simply print the article from the site, keep a written account of the incidents, or retrieve online news videos about the incidents. You can also start an online petition at: http://petitions.moveon.org/.

Many schools are unaware of bullying when it initially begins and will need proactive parents to report bullying as soon as it occurs. You can meet with or write administrators, teachers, or staff members to ensure they are aware of bullying in your school district. I'm a firm believer that school districts will turn a blind eye to multiple issues if it appears parents and families are not involved. If you become visible, the school district may become more active in protecting children in need.

Conclusion

his book has been a delight for me to write, although quite stressful. But my desire to write this book was based not only on my observations, but personal experience. Upon entering the field I began to feel confused about the ultimate purpose of my own profession because many people complained about the lack of care within the system. We must be reminded to see the mental health field as a "stop-and-go gas station," a place to get started on your journey of discovery. As a therapist, I research thousands of materials, many of which are difficult to retrieve without access to professional journals or archives, in order to educate families. I realize the big gap between what professionals know and what families know, so this book was written in hopes of narrowing this gap. Sadly, news is often hidden in local archives or small communities where it is difficult to see the vast number of people crying for changes. It wasn't until I reviewed a jury verdict in an archive that I learned about 28-year-old Fred Pisano, a man who murdered his mother in Mechanicsburg, PA and assaulted many others. In an attempt to downplay his violent outbursts, the community rarely heard of him. We are returning to the ways of the 1800s when unstable men were hidden in the basement of families too ashamed or fearful to reveal him. While striving to reduce stigma, we have compromised. This prevents us from openly discussing the tendencies of those unable to recognize their illness.

Violence does not characterize all individuals with complicated or severe mental health needs, but for those it does, we must discuss them with an open mind. This book is the beginning of an open, more informed discussion. While disappointed in multiple aspects of my field, I love what I believe is my life's calling. I am humbled when families share their lives with me. It is an honor. What makes a "helping professional" worthwhile is not their degree, long list of credentials, or schools they have attended, but their character and care of you. Remember to be keen to the quality of your therapist and theoretical orientation. Think about what the DSM is and how it is used. Engage in ways to offer a balanced perspective in your community and stay proactive. My mother always says "parenting is a journey, even with adult kids." So I often encourage self-care for many families. Be sure to make time for yourself – your mind, soul, and spirit. In order to help those you love, you need to develop your best side. Solitude, spiritual introspection, and anything that recharges you is what you need on a weekly basis. You don't want to burn-out. But most importantly remember to keep learning and take all you have learned in this book on your journey. I will be at the finish line rooting for you.

All the best to you and your family

REFERENCES

Anfang, A.S., & Appelbaum, (2006). Civil Commitment—the American experience. *Israel Journal of Psychiatry & Related sciences 43*(3), 209-218.

American Psychiatric Association. (n.d.). DSM-5 Research Planning Conference Summaries and Monographs. Retrieved from http://www.dsm5.org/Research/Pages/ConferenceSummariesand Monographs.aspx.

Beck, M. (2011, August 9). Confusing medical ailments with mental illness. *The Wall Street Journal: Health Journal*. Retrieved from http://online.wsj.com/article/SB1000142405311190448090457649 6271983911668.html.

Bentley, J.K., Rosenson, K.M., & Zito, M.J. (1990). Promoting medication compliance: Strategies for working with families of mentally ill people. *Social Work 35*(3), 274-277.

Belluck, P., & Carey, B. (2013, May 13). Psychiatry's guide is out of touch with science, experts say. *New York Times: Health*. Retrieved from http://www.nytimes.com/2013/05/07/health/psychiatrys-new-guide-falls-short-experts-say.html?_r=1&.

Bulloch, G.A., Adair, E.C., & Patten, B.S. (2006). Forgetfulness: A role in noncompliance with antidepressant treatment. *Canadian Journal of Psychiatry 51*(11), 719-722.

Christiana, N.G. (2013). 'Pieces of blade" found in stabbing victim. *ABC News*. Retrieved from http://abcnews.go.com/m/story?id=18922338&ref=http%3A%2 F%2Fnews.google.com%2F.

CBS Pittsburgh. (2013, February 26). Family of grandson accused in fatal stabbing speaks about mental illness. *KDKA*. Retrieved from http://pittsburgh.cbslocal.com/2013/02/26/family-of-grandson-accused-in-fatal-stabbing-speaks-about-mental-illness/.

Citizens Commission On Human Rights International. (2011, June 29). The problem with the DSM. Retrieved from http://www.cchrint.org/2011/06/29/the-problem-with-the-dsm/.

Center for Disease Control and Prevention. (2008). Youth Violence. Retrieved from http://www.cdc.gov/ncipc/dvp/YV_DataSheet.pdf.

Davies, J. (2013, May 6). Does your child really have a behavior disorder? A shocking book by a leading therapist reveals how millions of us-including children- are wrongly labeled with psychiatric problems. *Mail Online: Health*. Retrieved from, http://www.dailymail.co.uk/health/article-2320493/Does-child-really-behaviour-disorder-A-shocking-book-leading-therapist-reveals-millions--including-children--wrongly-labelled-psychiatric-problems.html.

Falchuk, E. (2009). Second opinion can save lives, cut costs. *Benefits & Compensation Digest 46*(10), 24-27.

Frances, A. (2013). *Saving normal*. New York, NY: HarperCollins.

Fine, M.J., & Acker, C. (1989, September, 11). When the struggle to help ends in death. *The Inquire Daily News: Philly.com*. Retrieved from http://articles.philly.com/1989-09-11/news/26103506_1_community-mental-health-system-group-homes-death.

Homeless Children Education's Fund. (n.d.). The "go-to" place for facts, figures, agencies, and useful websites. Retrieved from http://www.homelessfund.org/resources.html.

Huffington Post. (2013, April 11). Rehtaeh Parsons, Canadian girl, dies after suicide attempt; parents allege she was raped by 4 boys. *Huffington Post: Crime*. Retrieved from http://www.huffingtonpost.com/2013/04/09/rehtaeh-parsons-girl-dies-suicide-rape-canada_n_3045033.html?utm_hp_ref=mostpopular.

Lozano, A.J. (2013, April 11). Dylan Quick, Lone Star Community College stabbing suspect, due in court. *Huffington Post: Crime.* Retrieved from http://www.huffingtonpost.com/2013/04/11/dylan-quick-lone-star-community-college-stabbing-court_n_3059854.html.

Los Angeles Times. (2013, March 7). Court wont toss charges against ex-cop in Kelly Thomas death. *L.A. Now.* Retrieved from http://latimesblogs.latimes.com/lanow/kelly-thomas/.

National Alliance to End Homelessness. (n.d.). Issues. Retrieved from http://www.endhomelessness.org/pages/issues.

National Bullying Prevention Center. (2013). Bullying and harassment of students with disabilities. *PACER.* Retrieved from http://www.pacer.org/bullying/resources/students-with-disabilities/.

National Institute of Mental Health. (2010). Child and Adolescent Mental Health. Retrieved from http://www.nimh.nih.gov/health/topics/child-and-adolescent-mental-health/index.shtml.

Nelson, C. (2013). Narcissistic personality disorder: Not even a diagnosis in 2013! *The Journal Of Psychohistory 40*(4), 293-305.

Nelson, S. (2013, April 10). Texas stabber Dylan Andrew Quick was bullied, fantasized about murdering with knife, reports say. *US News.* Retrieved from http://www.usnews.com/news/newsgram/articles/2013/04/10/texas-stabber-dylan-andrew-quick-was-bullied-fantasized-about-murdering-with-knife-reports-say.

Oritz, E. (2013, April 10). Phoenix-area man kills wife and son after fears he contacted HIV from NY prostitutes. *New York Daily News.* Retrieved from http://www.nydailynews.com/ariz-man-kills-wife-son-fears-contracted-hiv-article-1.1312842.

Office Of Mental Health. (n.d.). Appendix 2: Kendra's Law: Assisted
     Outpatient Treatment In New York. Retrieved from
     http://www.omh.ny.gov/omhweb/kendra_web/interimreport/ap
     pendix2.htm.

Office Of Mental Health. (n.d). An explanation of Kendra's Law.
     Retrieved from
     http://www.omh.ny.gov/omhweb/Kendra_web/Ksummary.htm.

Owen, C., Rutherford, V., Jones. M., Tennant, C., & Smallman, A.
     (1997). II. Noncompliance in psychiatric aftercare. *Community
     Mental Health Journal 33*(1), 25-34.

Office For Civil Rights. (2012, September 21). Disability
     Discrimination. *U.S. Department of Education.* Retrieved from
     http://www2.ed.gov/policy/rights/guid/ocr/disability.html.

Pomeroy, C. E., & Parrish, E. D. (2012). The new DSM-5: Where have
     we been and where are we going? *National Association Of Social
     Workers 57*(3), 195-200.

Ringstad, R.. (2008). The ethics of dual relationships: Beliefs and
     behaviors of clinical practitioners. Families In Society: *The Journal
     Of Contemporary Social Services89*(1), 69-77. Doi:

Szabo, L. (2013, January 7). Committing a mentally ill adult is complex.
     USA Today. Retrieved from
     http://www.usatoday.com/story/news/nation/2013/01/07/ment
     al-illness-civil-commitment/1814301/.

Swartz, S. M., & Swanson, W.J. (2004). Involuntary outpatient
     commitment, community treatment orders, and assisted outpatient
     treatment: What's in the data. *Canadian Journal Of Psychiatry 49*(9),
     585-591.

Strang, S. (2009). Assisted Outpatient Treatment in Ohio: Is Jason's
     Law life-saving legislation or a rash response? *Health Matrix 19,*
     247-277.

Treatment Advocacy Center. (n.d). Consequences of nontreatment. Retrieved from http://www.treatmentadvocacycenter.org/problem/consequences-of-non-treatment.

Treatment Advocacy Center. (n.d). Homelessness: One of the consequences of failing to treat individuals with severe mental illness-backgrounder. Retrieved from http://www.treatmentadvocacycenter.org/index.php?option =com_content&task=view&id=1379&Itemid=217.

Treatment Advocacy Center. (2013). Fact Sheet: Modernize Pennsylvania's Civil Commitment Law. Retrieved April 4, 2013, from http://www.treatmentadvocacycenter.org/resources/mental-health-law/more-on-mental-health-laws/624. http://www.nimh.nih.gov/statistics/3AGES1865.shtml

Testa, M., & West, G. S. (2010). Civil commitment in the United States. *Psychiatry (Edgemont)* 7(10), 30-40.

Teplin, A.L., McClelland, M.G., Abram, M.K., & Weiner, A.D. (2005). Crime victimization in adults with severe mental illness: Comparison with the National Crime Victimization Survey. *Archives of General Psychiatry 62*(8), 911-921.

United States Department Of Justice. (2009). Addressing mental illness in the criminal justice system. The Justice Blog. Retrieved April 12, 2013, from http://blogs.justice.gov/main/archives/431.

Youth Violence: A report of the Surgeon Generals. Violence and mental health. (2009). Retrieved January 18, 2010 from, http://www.surgeongeneral.gov/library/youthviolence/chapter3/sec2.html#cooccure.

Suggested Resources

Mental Health Association of Pennsylvania	National Resource Center on Advanced Directives
http://www.mhapa.org/reso urces/MHAD.htm.	http://www.nrc-pad.org/ (click on "state by state")
Address: 1414 N. Cameron Street, 1st Floor Harrisburg, PA 17103 **1-866-578-3659**	

	U.S. Department of Health and Human Services
National Alliance On Mental Illness	http://www.hhs.gov/ocr/pri vacy/.
http://bit.ly/HODVw	200 Independence Ave SW Washington, DC 20201
Address: 3803 N. Fairfax Dr. Ste. 100, Arlington, VA 22203	
1-800-950-NAMI	Treatment Advocacy Center
	http://bit.ly/ZKX7U4
	Address 200 N. Glebe Road, Suite 730, Arlington, VA 22203
	707-294-6001

Index

A

American Psychiatric Association, 104

Americans with Disabilities Act of 1990, 170

    Authorization to release healthcare information, 28, 88

    Court-ordered treatment, 44, 80, 128, 130, 187, 188

B

Bachelor of Arts, 34

Bachelor of Social Work, 32

Bar Association, 47

Behaviroal problems and Bullying, 168

C

Children & Adolescents, 89

Civil commitment, 15, 56, 62, 129, 188

Civil Rights, 77, 170, 187

Criminalization, 120, 144

Cyber Bullying, 163

D

De-institutionalization, 16, 79

Diagnostic and Statistical Manual of Mental Disorders,18, 100

Doctor of Philosophy, 36

Doctor of Psychology, 36

E

Employee Assistance Program, 52

H

Health Insurance Portability and Accountability Act of 1996, HIPAA, 29

Holistic psychiatric care, 110

Homelessness, 62, 65, 144, 153, 159

I

Informed consent, 83

Table of Image Credits

Image Credits For Cover

African American girl with pink bow in hair
By Surachai, published on 20 July 2012
- Reference ID: 10093092
www.freedigitalphotos.net
Biracial family pose for self portrait
By photostock, published on 15 August 2011
- Reference ID: 10053475
www.freedigitalphotos.net
Hispanic Mother and daughter photo
By David Castillo Dominici, published on 14 November 2011
- Reference ID: 10064556
www.freedigitalphotos.net
Hispanic Pregnant woman praying
By David Castillo Dominici, published on 06 November 2012
- Reference ID: 100109910
www.freedigitalphotos.net
Hispanic Mother and son together
By David Castillo Dominici, published on 19 December 2012
- Reference ID: 100128234
www.freedigitalphotos.net
African American Mother and daughter
By David Castillo Dominici, published on 13 April 2012
- Reference ID: 10079951
www.freedigitalphotos.net

The Treatment Advocacy Center was mentioned in Chapter 4 of this book. Their media statement states that: "The Treatment Advocacy Center is a national nonprofit organization dedicated to eliminating barriers to the timely and effective treatment of severe mental illnesses. TAC promotes laws, policies and practices for the delivery of psychiatric care and supports the development of innovative treatments for and research into the causes of severe and persistent psychiatric illnesses, such as schizophrenia and bipolar disorder. They take no money from pharmaceutical companies."

About The Author

Támara Hill, MS is a therapist specializing in child, adolescent, and family mental health. She works with troubled youth who have behavioral and mood disorders adapt and utilize their strengths in the home, school, and community settings. Although she has worked with trauma and autism spectrum disorders, she gleans most of her expertise from working with parents, families, and caregivers. She has also previously worked with young adults and older adults suffering from a variety of psychiatric disorders. As a family consultant and an international media contributor, Támara aims to empower parents, families, and caregivers to gain further knowledge about the system. She brings her passion, personal, and professional experience to the topic of severe mental health. She currently lives in Pennsylvania with her family.

Connect with her at:

AnchoredInKnowledge.com (http://bit.ly/189jqVL), PsychCentral.com (blogs.psychcentral.com/caregivers), or in social media as "Therapisttee" at (Twitter & Pinterest)

www.ingramcontent.com/pod-product-compliance
Lightning Source LLC
Chambersburg PA
CBHW060909280326
41934CB00007B/1242